Praise for
Brie Arthur *and* Gardening with Grains

"Grains? In your landscape? You better believe it! ... Get ready for your worldviews — or at least your landscape views — to shift dramatically."

~ **Chip Hope**, Director, Appalachian State University Sustainable Development Teaching and Research Farm

"We rarely think of the beauty of agriculture. Brie Arthur's delicious book brings this beauty directly to us. Her personal delight in gardening with grains is infectious."

~ **Chris Woods**, former director and chief designer at Chanticleer, Wayne, PA, author, Gardenlust

"Brie is the ultimate horticultural game changer. ...bold, visionary, and yet at the same time, utterly practical. There is no one better than Brie to be a catalyst for gardening change."

~ **Anne M. Spafford**, MLA, Associate Professor of Landscape Design, Department of Horticultural Sciences, North Carolina State University

"Gardening with Grains is a book that needed to be written."

~ **Jere Gettle**, owner, Baker Creek Heirloom Seeds

"Brie Arthur is the one person this world needs now more than ever when it comes to gardening and growing! ...My go-to source for gardening wisdom."

~ **Joe Lamp'l**, Creator and Executive Producer, PBS's "Growing a Greener World," joegardener.com

"Brie Arthur recovers grain's proper role in landscape design, and its power as a symbol of the harmony of humans and the growing world."

~ **Dr. David S. Shields**, Distinguished Professor, University of South Carolina;
author, The Culinarians

"Brie has a contagious passion for pushing the limits of the role of edible plants in the landscape. "

~ **Matthew Ross**, Director, Continuing Education, Longwood Gardens

"In this era of rampant urbanization, Brie Arthur has reignited the cultural conversation around home landscapes and food."

~ **Kelly D. Norris**, Director of Horticulture and Education, Greater Des Moines Botanical Garden

"Brie Arthur is the real deal ...the cheerleader we need to inspire us to action."

~ **Pam Beck**, author, Best Garden Plants for North Carolina

"Brie Arthur has the vision that the landscape can be functional and food producing, as well as decorative. ...that the inclusion of non-traditional landscape plants can enhance the landscape for the benefit of home-grown food production and the local environment."

~ **Dr. Gary Bachman**, Mississippi State University Extension, Research Professor of Horticulture;
Host and Executive Producer, "Southern Gardening"

"If you read Brie's books or attend her lectures, you cannot help but be swept up by her extraordinary vision and energy — you will be planting veggies and barley the very next day!"

~ **Barbara Katz**, London Landscapes LLC , Washington, DC

"Brie Arthur's Gardening With Grains is filled with fascinating observations on the beauty, culture and use of a wide variety of grains coupled with brilliant recommendations for their creative integration into the residential landscape."

~ **Patrick Cullina**, Patrick Cullina Horticultural Design + Consulting , New York, NY

"Brie Arthur inspires us to grow more grains, which are as beautiful as they are tasty. She passionately demonstrates the usefulness of these plants and how they can be in everyone's garden (and kitchen)."

~ **R. William Thomas**, *Executive Director and Head Gardener at Chanticleer, Wayne, PA*

"Anyone who knows Brie knows we're talking about a lady on a mission for adventuresome horticulture. With this book, Brie marries fun backyard food production with smart landscape horticulture and throws in a dash of credible agronomy to make it all work. "

~ **Dr. David Creech**, *Regent's Professor and Professor Emeritus,*
Stephen F. Austin State University, Nacogdoches, TX

"Thanks go to Brie for sharing her enthusiasm for growing grains!"

~ **Ros Creasy**, *edible landscaping pioneer; author,* Edible Landscaping

"A volume that makes you fall in love with agricultural grains is long overdue. ...Brie says in this book what she tells us always — that we gardeners are radicals who can take control of our own spaces and thereby change the definitions of beauty."

~ **Jenks Farmer**, *plantsman, garden designer, horticulturist; author,* Deep-Rooted Wisdom

"If you love plants, there's nothing better than a new garden experiment. Brie opens the door to a whole new world of grains in which gardeners get to play with their food!"

~ **Leslie F. Halleck**, *horticulturist, author, green industry consultant*

Gardening
with
GRAINS

Dear Lucy —

December 2019

I HOPE THAT YOU ARE DOING GREAT!

GROW LIKE A #CRAZY GRAIN LADY ☺

WISHING YOU ALL THE BEST — Brie Arthur

Gardening
with
GRAINS

Bring the versatile beauty of grains
into your landscape

Brie Arthur

Author of *The Foodscape Revolution*

st. lynn's
press

Pittsburgh

Gardening with Grains
Bring the versatile beauty of grains into your landscape

ISBN-13: 978-1-943366-35-4

Library of Congress Control Number: 2019933549
CIP information available upon request

First Edition, 2019

St. Lynn's Press . POB 18680 . Pittsburgh, PA 15236
412.466.0790 . www.stlynnspress.com

Book design – Holly Rosborough
Editor – Catherine Dees

Photo credits:
All photos © Brie Arthur except for the following:
David Arthur – pages xv and 25; Sonya Harris (Chip and Brie) – page 21;
Elina Pelican – pages 27, 28, 40, 150, 152, 191; Lisa Roper – pages 38, 102, 107, 108;
Bent Jensen – page 46; Patrick Cullina – page 62; Jeff Lynch – page 91;
Preston Montague – page 130; Brenda Ridgeway – page 134.

Illustrations © Preston Montague:
pages 52, 55, 60, 65, 74, 85, 95, 109, 110

Printed in Canada
On certified FSC recycled paper using soy-based inks

This title and all of St. Lynn's Press books may be purchased for educational, business or sales promotional use. For information please write:
Special Markets Department . St. Lynn's Press . POB 18680 . Pittsburgh, PA 15236

10 9 8 7 6 5 4 3 2 1

TO ALL THE GARDENERS:

THOSE FROM THE PAST WHO HAVE
LEFT US A LEGACY OF WISDOM AND ETERNAL HOPE...

THOSE IN THE PRESENT WHO SERVE AND
NURTURE THE EARTH'S GIFTS...

AND THOSE IN THE FUTURE, WHOSE INFLUENCE
WILL SHAPE GENERATIONS TO COME:

MY GRATITUDE.

Table of Contents

PART THREE
In the Garden

PART FOUR
What's Your Pleasure?

Introduction

Greetings from my sunny front yard in Fuquay-Varina, North Carolina. It is late spring, and the cool season grains are beginning to dry, making their statement all the more vividly. On this particular day, the breeze is strong and the humidity low. The sun sparkles and the cloudless Carolina blue sky provides the perfect backdrop to reflect on my grain journey.

As I kneel on a soft patch of turf to inspect the wheat, I realize that grass is one of the last remnants of the "normal" landscape I inherited upon moving to my home in 2010.

A decade ago, I could never have imagined the possibilities this former tobacco field would bring.

The freshly mowed lawn serves as a lush green stage for the spring show of grains as they turn amber. The arching stalks of barley, oats and wheat wave in the breeze and glow in the sunshine. I'm daydreaming of what this space will look like in September when it is replanted with warm season grains such as corn, rice and sorghum. The possibilities are endless.

Today is a day to dream, give thanks and reflect with gratitude. It's a day to take note of the simple moments, like a bee buzzing overhead, and appreciate the beauty that surrounds me. It's a day for me to hope that my ramblings will influence others to take up this great hobby of gardening and to perhaps inspire a few folks to toss some grain seed into the earth and experience this same joy.

No question, I am more than a bit unconventional. Some may consider my style "natural," or even "chaotic," since a gardener's hand isn't always obvious in what I do. But in reality, these plantings are carefully planned, planted and managed from sowing to harvest. This diverse assortment of plants does not happen by accident. These dynamic colors and textures create a show that is visually intriguing and offers a compelling story and sense of place.

I've been a professional horticulturist and home gardener for twenty years. Early on, I learned that the only certainty is you will never stop learning from growing plants. No two seasons will ever be the same. Gardening is the opposite of Groundhog Day, which is why it is such a special way to spend your time. You will fall in and out of love with different plants over the years as your life and garden change. You will have more or less time to devote as your journey ebbs and flows, but I encourage you to experiment with new plants as often as possible and treasure the simple moments spent in your paradise.

If someone had told me even five years ago that I would be investing my time and energy into writing a book on grains I would have explained that "No, I am a woody ornamental propagator," and walked away. But then one day you wake up and try something new and your world gets that much bigger.

That is what *Gardening with Grains* is aiming to achieve. I hope you will consider things you haven't thought of before and challenge your creativity as a gardener. I want you to dream big, beyond your home and neighborhood and imagine the impact that we can all have on shaping and nourishing our communities. But most of all, I wish to whet your curiosity and invite you to grow something new, in a different context – and enjoy the process along the way.

– Brie –

PART ONE

the story

One

My Grain Journey

*L*ike most home growers, I started as a traditional flower enthusiast. Now, twenty years into my life as a gardener, my approach has evolved. Most importantly, I want my act of gardening to improve the environment in which I live. To do that, I have had to re-evaluate my use of fertilizers, herbicides and pesticides and prioritize soil improvement above all else. It was through these studies that I first became aware of grains and how valuable they could be for making my garden flourish, naturally.

To start this story I have to first explain how I came to be "the Crazy Grain Lady," with an 850-square-foot area of my front lawn turned into a grain bed. It didn't start off that way. In fact, when I was drawing plans for that initial

(non-grain) garden installation in my front yard, I simply sited a few favorite small trees in a sweeping line to mimic the contour of the foundation landscape. I had seen this technique used to create a screen and divide a lawn into two defined zones, one viewed from the street and the other a private area near the house. Considering that our suburban lot is deep and rather narrow, this seemed a logical way to maximize planting space without eliminating too much turf.

When we broke ground on the garden in January, 2011, the trees were planted as individual specimens, free standing and not connected by a bed. After a few months of trying to maintain the constantly spreading

Pink muhly grass thrives in my dry landscape beds.

NOTE: Not every landscape endeavor is meant to be a DIY project! In this case, we hired a landscaper with a turf cutter who expertly removed the sod in perfect sections, ready to be transplanted elsewhere. Sure, it cost money, but it was done correctly and completed in one day. Honestly, the turf would still be there if we had decided to make this a do-it-yourself project. Having worked in the landscape industry for a number of years, I have learned a few things about working smart instead of hard. I cannot stress this enough: Hire a professional for the jobs that seem too big for you to do yourself. There are a number of reasons for this – namely, professionals have access to the correct equipment for the job at hand, and they know how to use these tools and complete a job quickly.

centipede grass around them, my husband, David, and I decided it would be smarter to connect the tree wells with a small bed of native ornamental grasses, namely, *Muhlenbergia capillaris*, aka pink muhly grass. This would look beautiful and reduce our efforts to keep the turf from invading the roots of the newly planted trees. Plus, it was a native grass, so it would thrive, right? But first, we would need to dig up a lot of the invasive sod to make room for our muhly grass.

Aidan helped me measure the beds so they could be drawn to scale.

Once the sod was removed, I was left with a blank slate of bare sand. Have I mentioned I garden in a former tobacco field? Yes, I live on the sandy side of North Carolina, which has its benefits and drawbacks. One thing I never expected was how wet it would be living on sand. Sure, logically you think sand will drain fast, and yes that is true, unless you live where the water table is very high. Here, we live with the opposite of gravity, known as hydrologic pressure, meaning water comes from below. When the water table is saturated, the soil is too. It makes sense that all of the surrounding cities have the word "spring" in their name, as after a heavy rainstorm water will literally spring out of the ground.

This reality led to many plant deaths, because for too long I was trying to use my conventional wisdom about drainage. Of course, from failures come insights, even when it takes longer than it should, and I am an expert at doing things the wrong way! That first spring after planting the pink muhly grass, I watched in dismay as each plant went dormant and never returned to life. Upon closer inspection, the roots had simply rotted and my dream of a showy fall border faded away. But I still had my specimen trees in my otherwise empty bed. It needed something beautiful to complete the design, something that would survive the realities of my soil. What to do next?

ALWAYS HAVE A PLAN B: That may have been the first time in my gardening life that I felt like I had a black thumb. Now, I hate that term and I try to never use it, but the truth is, when you spend your hard-earned money on plants that

Chip Hope introduced me to grains by sharing a bag of wheat seed.

die, you feel like a failure. I struggled to come up with a plan B, until a chance meeting with Ros Creasy, my longtime role model and edible gardening guru. She was the first person to ever mention the idea of seasonal grains – and what a brilliant idea it was, although I didn't know it at the time. That came later, when my friend Chip Hope, a senior lecturer at Appalachian State University and Director of the ASU Sustainable Development Farm, handed me a bag of wheat seed and challenged me to grow it.

I have never looked back. ✍

I discover wheat

As a child growing up in the Midwest, I recall the faint shade of green in fields as the snow would melt, revealing the winter wheat that farmers had sown the prior autumn. It was a sign that spring would arrive – sometimes sooner than later. But beyond that insignificant observation, I never had to think about what came next.

Cheerios, Rice Krispies and oatmeal were staples for breakfast, and while I was amused by the cartoon mascots, I never once considered what I was eating or where it was grown. Like most people, I took for granted that grains were a part of my daily diet, filling me up and providing me with energy. I would devour macaroni and cheese, yet I was totally ignorant of an understanding of what pasta was. As far as I was concerned, it came from a box that was purchased at the grocery store. The end.

A DIGRESSION: Later in life, when I discovered the undeniably delicious flavor of beer, I was once again faced with the reality of ignorance. I hadn't considered what malted barley actually was; it was just decoration for the bottle's label.

As the "local" micro brewery scene expands across North America, does anyone ask, "Where was that barley grown?" or "How local is local?" Would beer drinkers even recognize a barley plant if they saw one?

But back to the wheat: I have a tendency to go overboard in the garden. What started off as a novel fascination quickly blossomed into a full-blown obsession. First of all, I had no idea wheat would be so pretty! Additionally, it was inexpensive and easy to grow. I quickly learned that wheat has a lot more to offer than just seasonal beauty.

MY FIRST GRAIN BED: As I was sowing that first crop of wheat seed, I didn't know what to expect. It was the middle of December and the Carolina temperatures were dropping quickly. I don't own a tractor, and as I prepared the space for that original suburban grain experiment I wondered if growing my own wheat was an effort in futility. What would I actually get out of it? Would my neighbors be offended? No one else was growing it, so there must be some reason why it has never been part of a landscape, at least in my lifetime.

The bed or "wave" as we call it, is situated in full sun and bisects the front yard. It runs about 100 feet long by 8 feet wide and still includes the choice trees, which create the taller screening from the road. Inspired by the Serpentine planting at Chanticleer Garden, this bed creates two distinct areas: a street-facing lawn and shrub border and our private garden space closer to the house. This arrangement allows me to experiment in a way that is a perfect crossover from traditional landscape

Did you know... wheat can improve your soil? The strong roots will break through compacted soil and act as a natural tiller! And what about using the hay as compost to improve your topsoil? Just mow the stalks in place and they will add essential organic matter that will feed your next crop. How about growing your own organic birdseed? Yep, grains do that too!

to agricultural cultivation. I am keen to keep the space tidy and be a good neighbor while providing a more conventional welcome for visitors.

Much to my surprise, the seed germinated quickly, popping through the bare earth as bright green sprouts, an amazing contrast to the tan of the dormant centipede turf surrounding the bed. Every day, I would stand in amazement as the seedlings grew stronger, unaffected by the nightly frosts. Within two weeks, the green was so dominate it looked like spring at Christmas.

The winter months passed and the wheat continued to thrive. With longer days and spring rains, it stretched toward the sky. One day, flower stalks appeared and gently waved in the wind as their pollen floated about, ensuring an abundant harvest was on the horizon.

SO MUCH BEAUTY: It wasn't until the wheat dried, which happened almost overnight, that I felt the strongest connection to God and country. Here in my suburban front yard, I had literal amber waves of grain, and I would bow down, camera in hand, totally fascinated by each seed that had developed. "America the Beautiful" would fill my head on repeat – and then I would stand at attention wondering, "What on earth do I do now?"

What I did was wake up very early in the morning, before the late spring temperatures rose into the 90s, and begin hand harvesting with my trusty Okatsune pruners. This was the most beautiful thing I had ever grown, so I carefully gathered each handful, wrapping a rubber band at the base, thinking of how I would make beautiful table arrangements with my newfound best friends. I had no intention of eating such a lovely plant! Five wheelbarrow loads and about a thousand Instagram posts later, I called my dear friend Erin Weston and declared I had her next product to offer at Weston Farms. Wheat would be the perfect complement to her gorgeous line of cut magnolia wreaths, garlands and bouquets. We both squealed with delight, as if we were the first people to ever discover the ornamental quality of a plant that has evolved for more than 10,000 years.

TOO BEAUTIFUL TO EAT? Of course, my logical, engineering-savvy husband decided we had to eat at least some of the harvest. New questions started to emerge: "How do we get the seed out? How do you refine it into flour?" Thus began the research on threshing, winnowing

My dear friend Erin Weston of Weston Farms was delighted with the wheat harvest!

and grinding and how to do it with a modern sensibility in the suburbs, sans a combine. The more we learned, the more my obsession began to take over my being. All of my social media posts now included the hashtag #CrazyGrainLady. I needed to store each and every photo to reference back at a future date.

As promised, David rose to the challenge and created a homemade thresher consisting of a paint bucket with a lid, a drill and a long rod with chain link attached to the end (photo on page 153). We used box fans to blow the chaff away and invested in a hand crank grinder to achieve the ultimate goal of flour – all for a few zero-food-mile tortillas. Now this was eating local!

Harvesting my first wheat crop using hand pruners.

"How much flour do you get?" That's the first thing people ask. Surprisingly, you can yield significant amounts of flour from small amounts of square footage. We average 15 pounds of whole grain, organic, ground flour from an 850-square-foot landscape bed in our front yard! This realization of yield combined with beauty made me really consider the potential of the sunny, suburban landscapes that sprawl across the globe.

I experienced so much joy from growing wheat it didn't seem fair that everyone wasn't enjoying this same satisfaction of this beautiful plant. Not to mention the ease of growing, which would surely leave every person with the confidence of a green thumb. But more than that is the fascinating history of the evolution of grains and people.

Did you know... human beings first evolved into settlements as a result of cultivating grains?

Admittedly, this is a lot of work, as many authentic experiences are. And though I would never expect most people to go to these lengths, I have been overwhelmed with the level of curiosity that people have expressed. I will also mention, if you are counting carbs and depriving yourself of your favorite meals, you can eat as much bread as you want if you grow your own wheat and then hand harvest, thresh and grind it – this is serious exercise!

In cultures across the globe, cereal crops are the defining characteristic for human settlement. Prior to the grain revolution, populations migrated seasonally, as hunting and gathering was the primary means of supplying food. When grain crops began to be cultivated, communities developed and the human experience was forever changed. Now fast-forward 10,000 years and observe the lawns of suburban developments, covering more than 180 million acres across the United States. I see this land as untapped opportunities, full of potential to be cultivated in a way that would reduce food miles, increase our ability to sustainably manage land, eliminate food deserts and improve the nutritional quality of the food that we all consume.

Throughout this process I couldn't help but wonder why a plant as beautiful and fundamental to life on earth as wheat would be absent from home gardens. How had novelty crops risen to commonplace while vital carbohydrates are ignored entirely by home gardeners and the local food movement?

POACEAE, THE GRASS FAMILY

Sometimes "grass" gets a bad wrap. Most people, including myself, take grass plants for granted. We eat them, we walk on them and of course we spend a lot of time mowing them! But here's something that you may not know: *Poaceae* grasses and cereal grains are the third most important source of oxygen after trees and algae. An acre of turf produces more oxygen than an acre of rain forest! The plants of this large family are an extraordinary element of life on earth, providing so much more than just green turf!

It was then when I realized that wheat and other *Poaceae* (aka grass family) crops are not fundamentally part of the local, organic food movement. How could that be? Every farm-to-table restaurant event I have attended served bread, pasta and rice, yet sadly, when I started to enquire about the localness of those essential ingredients I was met with blank stares. It turns out there just aren't many regional growers nowadays. In fact, these ubiquitous starches are outsourced from hundreds, if not thousands, of miles away and often have no certified organic verification. I began to reevaluate this expensive, sometimes pretentious movement that advertises the benefits of local, but delivers something far from it.

Here's a thought: *If every person in my neighborhood devoted just 1,000 square feet to grains (50 x 20 feet) we could supply our local bakery with over 1,000 pounds of organically grown, local flour. Alternative, gluten-free grains could also be grown to benefit the population suffering from allergies, intolerances and celiac disease. What would society look like if every neighborhood, office park, school and church played a role in the local food chain, simply by reducing the existing turf and making room for seasonal grain crops? I dream about things like this a lot.*

THE CRAZY GRAIN LADY ON A MISSION: I set out to answer my questions and gain knowledge through seasonal experiments and research. I bought every variety of wheat seed I could get my hands on. And then I had a giant light bulb moment: Wheat was only one of many grains I could produce. Barley, corn, millet, oats, rice, rye and sorghum were all perfect candidates for seasonal development throughout my one-acre suburban foodscape – as well as pseudo-cereal grains like amaranth, buckwheat and quinoa. How had I lived all these years without realizing the potential of grains and pseudo-cereal crops?

(In this book, I give primary attention to six of these grains: barley, oats and wheat for the cool season; corn, rice and sorghum for the warm season.)

That was truly the point of no return. Soon, every conversation started with "Have you ever grown grains?" followed by an enthusiastic description of every single quality they embrace. When I decided to write this book, I was met with funny looks, eye rolls and polite disdain. More than a few friends offered comments such as, "Sure Brie, you and the eight other people in the world that care about local wheat," and, "Don't you see, carbs make people fat! They are on their way out of the modern diet." Still, I persisted, because I knew this book needed to be written.

What I've learned since that first grain bed

There's more to report about my first experimental wheat crop, and in the years since with a whole variety of grains. Managing this garden bed space has proven to be very easy.

- **I sow twice a year,** once with cool-tolerant grain crops and again in summer with heat-loving varieties. The seed germinates in place and has dense ground cover, thus eliminating weed pressure. It is irrigated only when necessary and is managed with all-organic products. Compared to every other edible I grow, grains are the easiest and lowest maintenance, and visually provide the greatest impact. If I were to plant this space in a mix of traditional home garden vegetables like tomatoes, peppers and eggplant, it would require a great deal more time, attention and fertility. (This is not to say that I don't do my share of inter-planting with veggies and grains. They play well together!)

Sow densely to reduce weed pressure.

- **I cover the ground.** Another lesson learned over the years is the importance of engaging the entire ground plane with plants. This is truly the critical component for lowering overall maintenance and reducing the need for herbicides. You see, when all of the ground is covered there is limited opportunity for weeds to establish themselves. This is not a new idea, nor is it exclusive to food crops. In fact, this idea of ground plane coverage is the new mantra for modern-day landscaping, from bio-swales and green infrastructure design to annual beds maintained along the highway. If you really want to stop using herbicides you need to cover the open mulch space with plants of your choosing.

- **I bask in the beauty.** I love how grass-like plants create a dynamic landscape with kinetic appeal – another important aspect of the role grains play when used as garden accents. Like most people, I am attracted to these plants. I adore their structure, color, texture; watching them blow in the breeze instantly lowers my blood pressure. Though I am determined to focus on the utility that plants provide, I can't escape the draw of the aesthetic. And we shouldn't have to. This is not an either/or situation. One of the great advantages of being a gardener in the 21st century is we can explore the many attributes that a plant has to offer. Grains are no exception.

REINVENTING THE LANDSCAPE: What I love most about cultivating annual grains is the opportunity to reinvent the landscape beds twice a year. With thoughtful crop rotations and interesting plant combinations I can create high impact color and textural interest while growing something of meaningful harvest. This strategy will also improve the soil that I grow in. As a horticulturist, I strive to be practical in how I apply plants to the world around me. And that is exactly what grains provide: practicality, beauty and a will to live that even a certified black thumb can't kill.

It didn't take me long to expand past the wave bed and into my foundation landscape and property borders. Now, I plant seasonal grains in every sunny spot that is available. I am never disappointed by their performance and with each crop I learn new lessons on how to be a better steward to the Earth.

I sometimes wonder what my life would be like if I hadn't been handed that bag of wheat seed from my friend Chip. At the time I had no idea what a profound difference that seed would make to me as gardener. Before growing grains I struggled with poor soil and the disease and insect infestations that are symptomatic of this common issue. My plant palette, though diverse, was ordinary and there was nothing particularly unique about my design style. I spent countless hours watering and fertilizing, time that I would never be able to spare now as my career has evolved.

My identity will forever be woven with grains, which is why I am proud to be the Crazy Grain Lady. It is my sincere wish that by sharing my grain journey you too will take a chance, sow some seed and reap the harvest of these crops that have been essential to human evolution. ■

Two

What are Grains
and why should you grow them?

The truth is, you don't need to know much to successfully grow grains – I certainly didn't. Until I started researching for this book, I didn't know the difference between a seed and a cereal grain, let alone how legumes fit in. So just what is a grain? It is a fair question to ask in the midst of our 21st century's anti-carbohydrate world. I'd venture to say very few people would correctly define a grain without first doing an online search.

There are two main types of grains:
Cereals, the focus of this book; and
Legumes, such as soybeans and peanuts.

Generally, grains are characterized by their hard, dry "seed" (which sometimes has an attached hull or fruit layer but doesn't have to).

If that description doesn't clarify it, I understand! But I promise it has no bearing on your ability to grow these wonderful plants.

Rye seed heads drying in the sun.

WHEN IS A "SEED" NOT A SEED?

The difference between seeds and grains is rather complex. Technically, a seed is an embryonic plant covered in a seed coat. Sometimes this seed is edible, other times it is not. Seeds are formed after fertilization of a plant has taken place and the ovule has ripened. In contrast, a grain is actually a fruit harvested from plants in the grass family, *Poaceae*.

The main advantage grains offer as a nutritional source is their durability and long shelf life. Compared to starchy foods and tubers such as potatoes, grains are better suited for industrial agriculture because they can be mechanically planted and harvested. They can be stored for long periods of time in large quantities and shipped across the globe without spoiling. Grains can also be pressed into oil and milled into flour. Global commodity markets exist for all grains but not for tubers, vegetables and fruits.

THE BOTTOM LINE: Grains are the most important staple food in the world. As a staple, they are eaten frequently, often multiple times a day. Rice, corn and wheat are the most common and all can be grown in your sunny home landscape! Half of the grains cultivated around the world are harvested for human consumption.

One of the reasons grains are so important is because they are a valuable source of carbohydrates and vitamins. When paired with a protein-rich legume, you can create a very healthy diet. Some examples include corn and beans, rice and tofu, and my favorite childhood meal, wheat bread and peanut butter.

NOT JUST FOR HUMANS: Grains are an essential aspect of livestock nutrition. A third of the world's grain supply is fed to animals, from cattle and chickens to our pet cats and dogs. Cooking oils and alcohol both start from grains, not to mention the many industrial products that are created, including biodiesel.

Our home landscapes offer a way to grow grains, like corn, with ecological consideration.

Simply put, life would not exist as we know it without cereal grain production. Even the paleo diet involves grains, to feed the protein sources. At the end of the day, no person gets around grain consumption.

If you can grow anything, you can grow grains

Like many of our favorite garden plants, grains are annuals, meaning they have one growing season per year, yielding one crop. The term annual indicates that a plant will go through every life stage in one season: growth, maturity, seed set and death. In the case of grains (unlike fruiting crops like tomatoes and peppers), you harvest *after* the plant dies.

Generally speaking, grains like to be grown in full sun, with moist, well-drained soil that has a neutral pH. Basically, I just described the ideal condition for almost every single garden plant. Of course, grains are well adapted to adverse conditions, but the advantage of growing them in your home landscape is that you can provide the cultural conditions to maximize their growth. Trust me – compared to a petunia or tomato, grains are the easiest plants in the world to cultivate!

Barley grows with purple cabbage through the cool season in central North Carolina USDA Zone 7B.

TIMING AND CLIMATE: When growing a plant you have no experience with, timing will be the biggest challenge. The good news is that there are grains that can grow in almost every climate. Some grains prefer cool weather others prefer hot, tropical regions. That is why I have split the six grains featured in this book into two categories: cool season/short-day crops, and warm season/long-day crops.

Rye is a cold-tolerant grain commonly grown for animal feed.

COLD-TOLERANT GRAINS: These are the grains that are tolerant of cold, wet climates, which often coincide with winter, when the days are short. This category includes barley, oats and wheat – all of them winter crops in my North Carolina foodscape. They prefer to grow in cool soil and air temperatures. They ripen as the days turn hot and long. In the northern U.S. and into Canada, barley, oats and wheat are frequently sown in very early spring and can grow through the duration of summer, with a fall harvest. However, some varieties of these plants are seeded in fall; they germinate but remain mostly dormant through winter and are harvested in late spring. Every region is different, which is why consulting a local authority is the very best advice I can offer.

HEAT-TOLERANT GRAINS: Warm season grains, such as corn, rice and sorghum prefer hotter soil and air temperatures. In North America, that is the condition of the long days of summer. In tropical regions, however, these plants can thrive year-round if adequate water is available. Most importantly, warm season crops need a soil temperature above 55°F for seed germination and root development. In my North Carolina garden I plant these varieties in May-June and harvest in early-mid fall.

Since I live in a subtropical climate (USDA Hardiness Zone 7) with four distinct seasons and mild winters, I am able to cultivate grains 12 months of the year. If you live in northern regions, the growing season is more condensed and planting dates will vary from early spring through mid-fall. As is the case with all plants, it is best to do some research on your specific growing area. I try to pay attention to what the farmers around me are doing. They earn their living from successfully cultivating crops, so they know when to plant and harvest.

Did you know ... warm season grains (like corn, rice and sorghum) are frost sensitive? They suffer when temperatures are below 40°F and can't survive below 32°F.

GREAT GARDEN COMPANIONS: As landscape elements, grains are well suited to be incorporated with other plants, both edibles and ornamentals. Although typically grown as monocultures in agricultural applications, in the home garden you can be more creative. I always say straight lines are for machines, so it is your job as a home grain grower to select companion plants based on cultural requirements in the space you have available. Sure, you can grow any of the plants featured in this book the way a farmer does, but why? The point here is that you are not a farmer, so give yourself permission to do something more interesting!

I love pairing my cool season grains with flowering annuals such as larkspur, poppies, nigella, bachelor's buttons and snapdragons. Warm season combinations include cosmos, marigolds, sesame, sunflowers and zinnias. The sky is the limit when it comes to pairing your grains with other garden specimens. (Chapter 8 will be all about beautiful companions for your grains.)

Beyond the sheer beauty and versatility of grains, I'm absolutely sold on how low maintenance they are – especially as I find myself traveling more and more and having less time in my garden. Grains require very little effort, including fertilizer needs, making them a great option for gardeners looking for less work.

Soil health is critical for successful plantings

I always recommend first getting a soil test to better understand what nutrients you may be lacking in your native soil. Once you have that information, you can start to layer organic matter in your beds.

GREEN MULCH: Here's another gift from the grain gods: growing grains for their biomass, which can be mowed in place after you harvest the seed. This "green mulch" practice is similar to cover cropping and offers a quick and easy solution for compacted ground, hardpan clay and even dry, sandy soil, by adding essential organic matter into the ground layer. Decomposition is really the key to feeding the soil's biology, and that will in turn feed your plants.

> ### MY FAVORITE NATURAL AMENDMENT IS GROUND LEAVES!
>
> Leaves truly are God's gift to gardeners, so don't rake them to the street or burn them. Instead, mow or shred them and topdress your beds. They will quickly break down and add nutrients to your soil.

> *Did you know* ... a plant's biomass is the combined weight of its plant material above and below the ground? Plant biomass can be valuable as a storehouse of the sun's energy gained through photosynthesis.

CROP ROTATION: Grains are frequently included in agricultural crop rotations as a means of building soil health, suppressing specific diseases and pests and adding nutrients back to the earth. This was a common practice in the pre-chemical era of farming, and I hope to see a resurgence of thoughtful crop rotations in the future. In particular, I want to encourage home growers to adopt this practice, as it is an easy way to improve the space you are growing in. Remember, there is no rule that says you can't apply a farming technique to your home landscape, just like there is no requirement for you to plant in straight lines when you are hand planting and harvesting!

To that end, cereal grains are ideal cover crops because their deep roots literally scavenge for nutrients. Essentially, as the grain develops, the roots seek out nutrients deep in the earth and draw them back to the surface through the stems and leaves. Barley, oats and wheat are particularly useful scavengers, providing natural fertility for the next season.

If I have said it once in my talks to gardeners, I've said it a thousand times: **Healthy soil results in happy plants, less disease and reduced insect pressure – and higher yields for you and your loved ones to enjoy.**

Some useful botanical definitions
(you will not be tested on this)

Understanding exactly what a cereal grain is may not seem important, but often people, including myself, find themselves confused. I want to take this opportunity to very generally explain the various categories and terminologies so you can feel like an expert!

Plants are first distinguished by their structure in the *cotyledon* stage, which simply refers to how many leaves appear upon germination. There are plants that will develop only one leaf, commonly referred to as a *monocot* and others that will have two leaves known as *dicots*.

MONOCOTYLEDONS are defined as flowering plants such as grasses, lilies and palms that have a single vein in the seed. Upon germination, a single leaf will appear. Monocots also share a combination of characteristics, including leaves with parallel veins and flower parts in multiples of three. They also lack secondary growth, which means they have a single growing point and do not "bush out" if you break the top off; this is known as "apical dominance," where the stem of the plant grows more strongly than other side shoots. Traditional grains are monocots.

DICOTYLEDONS include many of the most common garden specimens like tomatoes, peppers, potatoes, beans and peas. They are flowering plants that have two seed leaves and typically have flower parts in multiples of four or five and pollen with three pores. The leaves have reticulate venation (web-like veining) and they also have the capacity for secondary growth. This is why you can prune the tips of plants to induce a bushy growing habit.

PSEUDO-CEREAL GRAINS are starchy grains from broadleaf plant families; they are dicots. This includes amaranth, buckwheat, chia and quinoa. These tend to be easy-to-grow warm season crops that can set millions of seeds – which can become a problem for the home grower. Amaranth in particular can become quite a garden pest, difficult to eradicate. If you are inclined to grow it, I recommend harvesting the seed early to avoid the potential for a future invasion.

Buckwheat is a pseudo-cereal in the **Amaranthaceae** *family.*

Peanuts make a wonderful addition to the landscape (top photo), in addition to being a nutritious crop.

Rapeseed planted at Chanticleer is an oilseed grain.

GRAIN LEGUMES, also called pulses, are members of the pea family *(Fababceae)* and offer high protein content, ranging from 20-40%. These plants are dicots. In addition to being a source of protein, legumes also contain carbohydrate and fat. Delicious crops such as chickpeas, beans, lentils, peanuts, peas and soybeans are considered legumes. Grains and legumes are ideal companion plants and should be utilized in regular crop rotations to maximize the available nutrients in your soil. Legumes are nitrogen fixers; in addition to being important sources of nutrition, they also increase fertility in the soil.

OILSEED GRAINS are primarily grown for the extraction of their edible oil, fuel or lubricant. Many plants fall into this category, though most home gardeners grow them for their foliage and flowers. Mustards and rapeseed (the source of Canola oil) from the *Brassicaceae* family are important oilseed plants. Others include flax, hemp, poppy, safflower, sesame and sunflowers.

All of these plants grow in similar conditions to traditional cereal grains. I encourage you to consider growing these to complement your traditional landscape and expand your horizons. Even if a plant seems impractical from a harvesting perspective, that's okay! As home gardeners, we have the privilege of growing plants simply for the experience. Even a novelty crop can provide valuable educational opportunities as well as fascination and exposure to something out of the ordinary. ■

The Entwined History of Humans and Cereal Grains
(briefly told)

I am going to start this chapter with something I said in the last chapter (I feel it's that important): People and society as we know it today would not exist without the evolving cultivation of grains. Regardless of where you stand on the subject of consumption of cereal grains, this point cannot be ignored: Homo sapiens and grains co-evolved, and human life on this planet would not be as it is without this interaction.

If you will permit me a small rant: It drives me crazy as we endure an era where the fundamental value of cereal grains is minimized and dismissed in our diets. It has become just too easy to blame the carbs in grains for our increasing waistlines while disregarding the issues of processed foods. These times find us at odds with the vitally important concept of eating nutrient-dense foods, and instead offer fast, less nutritious alternatives at the expense of our health. We seem to have a serious disconnect between nutrition and long-term wellness. This hasn't happened overnight. It has followed closely on the increased industrialization and mass marketing of food production – along with our increased separation from the sources of our food. I suppose blaming bread and our genes is the easiest approach, but that's hardly the whole picture.

SO, WHAT *IS* ˙THE FUNDAMENTAL VALUE OF CEREAL GRAINS˙? At the early stages of human evolution, grains were there to provide much-needed caloric intake for our ancient ancestors. Cereals are a rich source of vitamins, minerals, proteins, carbohydrates, fats and oil. Grains were cultivated not only as food for people, but to provide energy for grazing animals and to improve soil health. Yet, in this era where people are so far removed from where their food is grown, grains have been turned into an enemy rather than a resource for healthy living.

It is generally believed that people first began eating grains at least as far back as 75,000 years ago in the Middle East. These grains, including einkorn and emmer wheat, were ancestors of today's *Triticum* species. Both einkorn and emmer grew wild near the banks of rivers, where people harvested the grasses that grew naturally near their communities long before "farming" techniques were established. Scientists believe they have discovered the world's oldest-known grain silos at an Early Neolithic village called Dhra', in modern Jordan. These silos, dating back 11,000 years, contained remnants of barley and early types of wheat. Another site, in Israel, revealed a trove of 23,000-year-old grains.

Over time, grains and their cultivation were becoming essential to the rise of civilization in other places around the world: rice in China, more than 8,000 years ago; sorghum in Africa, about 7,000 years ago; and in Mesoamerica, an ancestor of corn was domesticated about 6,000 years ago.

Ancient people ate grains in much the same way we do today. Wheat grains were made into flour and used for bread baking. Rice was steamed and eaten hot or cold. Oats were mashed with water or milk to make oatmeal. And perhaps most importantly, our ancient ancestors created beer by fermenting barley. Beer is the oldest manufactured beverage in the world and had very low alcohol content in its original creation. It too was an important source of carbohydrates and nutrients in ancient diets.

Did you know... there are records of the workers who built Egypt's pyramids at Giza being paid in beer and bread? An ancient example of grain being used by early civilizations as a form of currency.

The historical impact of grains in global agriculture is profound. Because grains are small, hard and dry, they can be stored, measured and transported easily, especially compared to other food crops like fresh fruits, roots and tubers. The development of cereal grains allowed excess food to be produced and stored, which ultimately led to the creation of the first permanent settlements and, in time, societal structuring.

Today, those of us living in the industrialized world take for granted that grains are grown, stored and transported across the globe. We are accustomed to seeing silos and giant combines responsible for efficiently harvesting crops. The invention of the combine created the single most important piece of agricultural equipment.

THE AMAZING COMBINE

The combine is truly a remarkable machine. It does three jobs in the harvesting of grain: cutting it, threshing it, and winnowing the seed from the chaff.

Cutting removes the grain from the stalk of grass. When doing this by hand in your home garden, it is just the removal of the seed head from the dried stem.

Threshing loosens the edible grain from its casing, called the chaff. The chaff is inedible and humans and animals cannot digest it. This step is significantly more complex for a home gardener without proper equipment, though there are some creative solutions for this step that involve your favorite child garden helpers! My young helpers have been threshing heroes.

Winnowing, the final step, is the removal of the grain from the chaff.

Combine harvesters make this process time- and cost-effective. It is my dream that one day there will be a combine for small-batch growers like me – and maybe you! (See page 153 for how we thresh and winnow at home).

HARVESTING ON A SMALL SCALE: The sight of those giant combines may be common in developed, wealthier countries, but the standard for global grain production isn't large fields tended by expensive machinery and planted with modern, genetically improved varieties. In the developing world today, very few farmers have the resources that we are so accustomed to seeing in North America. Farmers in the developing world typically cultivate just a few acres and provide grain for their local community. These farmers usually thresh and winnow with separate machines after harvesting the field. In many places, harvesting is still done with hand tools such as the sickle, a long, curved blade used for cutting many stalks of grain at once. These are the methods that home grain growers can look to as resources.

QUESTIONS ARISE: And this is why writing this book matters. For most of my life I took for granted the benefits of large-scale commercial agriculture, with its high efficiency and low cost. A modern miracle, no doubt, but it may be bringing unintended consequences. As scientists develop improved crops, we see agricultural practices evolve – the most controversial practice being the application of persistent herbicides and systemic pesticides (see Chapter Four).

Could some agricultural practices be negatively affecting health? It's a question that needs to be raised and settled. In the years to come, I hope and expect that will happen, and more information will be discovered regarding the rise of gluten intolerances and serious diseases like celiac. I do not want to speculate without proper data about conventional agricultural practices, and I encourage you to not rush to judgment on this topic either. But be mindful of what you eat and seek to learn about how it was grown. For me, my simple solution is to grow some of my own grains and support local farmers who cultivate a diverse range of crops, using organic methods whenever possible.

The act of gardening is meaningful. By growing the plants that you love to eat you impact more than just your own diet. You can influence your neighbors and create habitat for local insects and wildlife. The roots of your plants will help clean storm water. And every single time you eat something that you grew, you help reduce food miles. Gardening is a hobby that provides untold environmental benefits and solutions. I hope you will always remember that you are doing your part to make the world a better place, one plant at a time! ■

Ancient Grains to Modern-Day Cultivation

Ancient grains are a whole subject unto themselves and have recently garnered a fair amount of attention. The term conjures up a kind of exotic appeal, a return to a purer state, in tune with grains' essential nature. And yet, it's not a term that has a fixed meaning. With interest in ancient grains on the rise, it is important to examine what it does mean.

Since all cereals are technically ancient (having historical and archeological relevance dating back thousands of years), how can some be called ancient and others not? The current distinction relates to the purity of the strain. Generally, the term "ancient grains" refers to crops that are largely unchanged over the last several hundred years of cultivation. They have not been manipulated through commercial hybridization or genetic modifications. They

therefore replicate the *germplasm* – the genetic material of germ cells – that would have been grown in ancient times.

When people inquire about "ancient grains," they are most often referring to wheat – specifically, the varieties of einkorn, emmer (or farro), khorosan (or Kamut) and spelt.

Beyond wheat, heirloom varieties of other proper cereal grains such as black barley, red and black rice, blue corn, sorghum and millet are also classified as ancient grains. To make this even more intriguing, pseudo-cereal crops such as amaranth, buckwheat, chia and quinoa are also considered to be ancient grains. Obviously, this is a broad category full of complications, contradictions and the potential for misinformation.

WHAT ABOUT HEIRLOOMS? The term heirloom is always a cause of confusion. In my mind, it is an open-pollinated plant that pre-dates 1930. It isn't necessarily "ancient," in that these varieties marketed as heirloom are not thousands of years old. As I have researched the term "heirloom"– not only for grain but also in reference of the ever-so-popular category of tomatoes – the defining characteristics revolve around the idea that these are old varieties that are no longer in mainstream production. As a result, they are perceived to be more valuable, boasting better flavor and higher nutritional density. Those assumptions are not always accurate, which is part of the problem with terms like "heirloom" or "ancient" being used to market food crops. It is fair to say that both terms refer to old varieties that stir romantic notions of the past.

That is not to say there isn't great nutritional value in these olden-times selections. Ancient wheat berries are lower in gluten and higher in protein and micronutrients. Einkorn, for example, has a higher concentration of beta carotene compared to modern varieties. In the end, like all things, it is your job as the consumer to do your research and gain a better understanding about the food you eat every day.

> ## ANCIENT WHEAT VARIETIES AND THEIR BOTANICAL NAMES:
>
> **Einkorn** – *Triticum monococcum*
> **Emmer or Farro** – *Triticum dicoccum*
> **Khorosan** or **Kamut** – *Triticum turanicum*
> **Spelt** – *Triticum spelta*

I experiment with ancient grains

The first cereal crop I grew was not an ancient variety. The grain that Chip Hope challenged me to cultivate was a hard red spring wheat called 'Glenn', which was introduced by North Dakota State University. To say the least, it was a resounding success that left me full of confidence in my grain growing ability. After that, and because I'm a born experimenter, I was determined to try my hand at varieties that felt more authentic – some ancient grains. Just thinking about it made me happy. I enjoy cultivating Old World plants as a means of connecting to times long past. That is one of those privileges we modern gardeners can indulge in, because we are not depending on these crops as our sole source of nutrition.

Seed of ancient grains, specifically wheat, was readily available from my beloved heirloom sources, so access was just a few clicks away. Naturally, I ordered ten packs of every variety listed and took to the garden in a fit of glory and excitement.

Since I cherished these seeds, I was careful to sow them exactly according to the instructions. These ancient grains would occupy the most prized real estate in the garden. Every week I logged their progress, taking thousands of photos to document their growth. I was loving it!

AND THEN... Winter can be a difficult season no matter where you live. Temperature fluctuations and snow all wreaked havoc on my freshly germinated sprouts. After a sudden low in the single digits and sustained temperatures below freezing, entire crops melted to the ground, composting in place, never to be seen again. The crushing reality of why modern hybrids were created started to seep into my awareness.

As temperatures began to warm up, the remaining ancient grains sprang to life and reignited my dream of self-sufficiency the old-fashioned way. Then, much to my dismay, I watched as a strong wind and thunderstorm blew my ancient crops to the ground.

Initially, I thought it was no big deal. Surely, upon drying they would perk back up. But alas, they did not. That was my first experience with crop lodging, meaning the stem broke at the base and flopped over. I lost more than 80% of my ancient grains that spring and I learned a valuable lesson: **Do not dismiss the importance of science, genetic improvements and the evolution of plants.**

Online retailers have a wide variety of ancient grain seed.

A ripening field of wheat in Denmark.

It is experiences like this that result in the best lessons learned. First, I developed an appreciation for the challenges people faced in earlier times. It became clear to me how famines could occur – one storm could wipe out an entire region's crops. Ancient varieties simply lack the necessary structural integrity to hold up, even in my small residential plot. This experiment also provided me a new perspective and appreciation for modern crops. Genetic improvements in our global food supply should not be entirely perceived as negative. Scientists work tirelessly to breed for practical improvements, including disease and insect resistance and higher yields. To dismiss the progress of modern breeding is a true injustice to science, and is simply not realistic when looking at the big picture of global agriculture.

I'm not saying that ancient grains should be written off for the home gardener or the dedicated local farmer with a strong belief in those "source" grains. I applaud and respect anyone who can bring a healthy crop to maturity. As a home grain grower, I am not giving up on cultivating ancient varieties. I am growing them alongside modern selections, as I believe there is a place for them all. What matters most to me is HOW they are grown – organically and never sprayed with pesticides or herbicides. In my opinion, growing practices are the important consideration.

A GOOD WORD FOR MODERN CULTIVARS: One of the many advantages of modern cultivars of wheat and other grains is the added structural integrity they possess. This means they can withstand normal to extreme weather events and not lodge (break at the base). They also yield at higher rates and have better resistance to disease, fungus and pests, making these modern hybrids all the more user friendly. It makes sense that for large-scale production ancient grains are not a viable consideration.

To be clear, I am a horticulturist and landscape designer by education and training. I am not a geneticist, plant breeder or botanist, and my purpose here is not to mount a scientific-data defense or denunciation of ancient grains against their new-age counterparts. But rather than focusing on the purity of variety, I believe that the *cultural growing methodologies* and the processing of the grains are the most important aspects leading to a nutritional differentiation.

Did you know... "cultural growing methodologies" refers specifically to how a crop was cultivated? Was it grown with organic practices or by conventional means? Specifically, were the plants treated with synthetic fertilizers, pesticides, fungicides and herbicides?

As a horticulture professional, I put my trust in scientific data and rely on that to guide my decision making. It is imperative that I recognize that as a home gardener I have no expertise on the subject of food safety with regard to chemical applications. Researchers and scientists share the burden of analyzing health risks against the advancements and efficiencies that breeding modifications and synthetic chemistry provide. In an industry focused on feeding a global population of 10 billion by 2050, scientific advancements in crop production appear to be the only sustainable solution. This includes plants that are genetically modified to be resistant to herbicides. The application of synthetically derived fertilizers and pesticides is also a reality that should not be ignored.

BUT... Throughout my life, the environment has been under attack. It pains me that environmental considerations have become politicized, as if all humans don't suffer the same when the Earth is contaminated. Growing up in Michigan, water quality was always a concern, and clearly remains so as we see ongoing struggles in communities like Flint.

Some questions to ponder: What role do agricultural products play in contamination of our precious resources? Are "best practices" being fully utilized? How can we improve productivity and ecological systems?

To me, there is an aspect of our current agricultural model that seems short sighted, specifically with regard to modifications that allow the crop to be resistant to herbicide applications. I totally understand the need to control weed pressure and appreciate that this method actually reduces the number of herbicide applications – but I have to ask: *Is spraying millions of acres of land with a synthetic herbicide that impacts the soil health and ultimately leaches into waterways the best solution for food production?*

Let's be honest: Glyphosate would not be the first chemical that was initially considered safe until years later, when scientists proved it wasn't. Think back to the invention of asbestos and DDT at the start of the chemical revolution. Now, many substances are banned. Will that be the case in 20 years with our current round of "agriculture-safe" chemistries?

I am cautiously optimistic that conventional agricultural methods are in fact safe, but we cannot deny the many instances where a product is eventually linked to health issues. I suppose only time will tell the long-term impact of our consuming systemic and persistent herbicides such as glyphosate, clopyralid and aminopyralid.

It is important to be a critical thinker and spend time reviewing studies and dissecting data to become part of the solution. I am motivated to help develop creative strategies for the challenges of the future through the act of growing food in a meaningful way. That requires having an open mind to scientific advances while looking to the past to seek wisdom.

IT'S COMPLICATED: If I have learned anything in researching for this part of the book it is that 1) this is a hot topic, and 2) there is no simple solution. Consumers have a serious deficit of practical knowledge on the subjects of food science, genetic modifications, soil health and chemistry. And global biotech companies have lost our trust due to their lack of transparency. Farmers are challenged to grow food in the most efficient way possible to feed the world, and consumers demand low prices. There is a lot about our current agricultural model that could be reevaluated. Health starts with consumption, and most of us have at least some control over what we eat.

As a person who has struggled for two decades with food intolerances, I am genuinely concerned that our reliance on synthetically derived compounds may be impacting our

Growing my own grains has increased my appreciation for farmers around the world.

body's ability to digest. It seems logical to assert that if synthetic chemistries destroy soil health, they may also have the same effect on our gut health. Not being a nutritionist, I will equate this to a subject I am better educated in: soil science.

FERTILIZER AND SOIL HEALTH: One of the main differences between organic and conventional growing is conventional growing's use of synthetic, often sodium-based fertilizers. As they penetrate the earth, the microbial activity is disturbed, influencing the natural cycles of ammonification and nitrification of bacteria, which would naturally feed the plant roots. In contrast, with organic growing methods, which are easily adopted by home gardeners, you can focus on soil health – so put the blue stuff down! There is a mountain of research available to show the benefits of focusing your gardening efforts first and foremost on soil health, to increase fertility the natural way.

In published research by the American Society of Agronomy, the addition of manure and other composted organic matter was found to support and improve soil quality in many ways. Here are just some of the research results:

- Manure and other composted organic matter managed the balance of soil pH, a measure of acidity or alkalinity. (Inorganic – aka synthetic – fertilizer makes the soil more acidic.)

- Organic matter improved organic carbon, which means better soil structure.

- Organic matter increased total nitrogen, which is key to plant growth.

- Organic matter amplified water-stable aggregates, which are groups of soil particles that stick to each other. This helps soil resist water erosion. (Inorganic fertilizer application decreased these aggregates.)

Simply put, inorganic fertilizer is not the best way to grow, especially for home gardeners who are managing less land than agricultural growers, and who can devote more time and energy to building quality soil. It's their personal investment in the health of their soil.

Other research indicates that many food sensitivities (though not allergies or celiac disease) may actually be related to our inability to break down compounds found in commonly used inorganic products, specifically herbicides and pesticides. For me, this is motivation to grow some of my own foods.

GMOS: While I am broaching this rather loaded subject, the discussion of genetic modifications must be addressed – yet another issue that people need to become better educated about.

Did you know ... Genetically engineered (GE) and genetically modified (GM) are interchangeable terms that refer to varieties of crops developed by means other than traditional breeding? (the National Academy of Sciences)

Technically speaking, a genetically modified organism can be created through a range of methods including selection, hybridization and induced mutation. This results in an alteration of the genetic composition to achieve a desired result. Genetic engineering is the direct manipulation of an organism's genome using biotechnology.

Most people think GE means moving genes from one species to another, or transgenic manipulation – like spider DNA inserted into corn. That is not exclusively the case. Gene editing is an important aspect of DNA manipulation. That can involve deletion, insertion, silencing or repression of genes in a plant. Sometimes, genes from closely related species are used, creating cisgenic plants. The main thing to know: cisgenic changes to DNA would be possible through conventional breeding, while transgenic changes are not possible without biological technology.

The science of crop improvements is complicated, as I mentioned, and while I am weary of modifications that enable specific chemistry applications (such as Roundup Ready corn and soy), many genetic alterations help reduce inputs by making selections for improved flavor and nutrient density, disease and pest resistance, drought tolerance and increased yields.

The bottom line is this: We all need to engage in an intelligent conversation based on the best scientific facts available, not emotions or assumptions, so we can ensure a future with safe, ethically grown food crops.

PROCESSING AND NUTRITIONAL VALUE:

Nutritional values are one means of identifying a superior variety. Often, people consider ancient grains to be more nutritious than New World hybrids. However, this is a topic that really revolves around how the grains are processed.

Whole grains have more nutrition than refined grains, like the white flour that is used for an overwhelming amount of common foods. Healthy, whole-grain alternatives are not exotic or expensive. Consider brown rice, whole-grain pasta, oatmeal, popcorn and whole-wheat bread as nutrient-dense, affordable dietary selections. The critical point here is to recognize that less processing means increased nutritional value.

Overall, ancient grains are providing an important platform for a discussion that is long overdue. In a world where critical thinking struggles to exist, why not use your garden as a means of educating yourself and others? The opportunities to cultivate your own laboratory and testing ground are boundless and you may discover insights that you would otherwise overlook. I for one want to be a part of the solution for a brighter, more healthful future, and I believe growing grains is an important part of making that a reality. ∎

PART TWO

the grains

Five

Three Great Cool Season Grains
Barley • Oats • Wheat

The three cool season cereals featured here include barley, oats and wheat. From a landscape perspective, all offer the same dynamic textural appeal and require the same cultural growing conditions: full sun, cool temperatures, moist but well-drained soil that is rich with organic matter.

Since these varieties grow through the cool season, they require very little supplemental irrigation, something I appreciate greatly. Depending on the variety you grow and where you live, these crops will be planted in late fall or early spring and take about six months to mature. The reason I love cool season grains is because they grow all winter in my home landscape, brightening an otherwise dull time of year. Since I grew up in the cold, snowy North, anything that is green and actively growing through the winter seems like a miracle! I cherish the sight of the newly sprouted leaves and watch with delight and anticipation as they develop.

Barley – The Beauty Queen
Horedeum vulgare

Barley

Introduction

I first grew a small batch of barley in the winter of 2015. Like the others grains I was experimenting with, it germinated quickly in the cooling soil of late autumn. Greens sprouted, breaking through the soil surface in less than a week, and rapidly developed into wide, lush blades of foliage. It had a vigor that exceeded the other cool season grains I had sown on the same day, as if it was determined to show off immediately. Barley caught my attention on that early December day and it remains the "beauty queen" of the cool season cereals that I cultivate.

Originally, I grew barley as a novelty, simply because I came across an inexpensive pack of seeds and had recently become enchanted by the likes of wheat and oats. It didn't even occur to me as I sowed those first seeds that barley had a storied past and played an important role in the development of modern society through my favorite adult beverage, BEER!

As microbreweries open in every community, I think there is an opportunity to cultivate small batches of local barley to supply these businesses. It was for this reason that barley caught my attention, as it seems more practical to make beer than to grind flour! It got my wheels turning: What if barley was included as a landscape feature and then used as a truly local ingredient at these nearby breweries?

The talented gardeners at Chanticleer Garden* recognized the aesthetic qualities of barley. In the spring of 2018 they sowed a massive display in the Serpentine border. As the malted barley germinated, the bright green, finely textured leaves sprouted neatly, ultimately growing to three feet tall. As the days grew long, the crop turned golden. The contrast against the surrounding lawn caught the attention of every visitor. *(To see more of Chanticleer's inspirational grain landscapes, turn to pages 91, 102, 107 and 108.)

Even if you don't have room for a large display, you can grow barley in a container as a seasonal annual "thriller" or as clumps in the landscape. Think of it as an annual ornamental grass. When it ripens, simply cut it and display it in a vase with no water. You can also add the dried stalks and flowers to holiday arrangements or use them throughout the year as a unique homegrown decoration.

SOIL BENEFITS: I also grow barley to improve my native soil. When mowed in place, the chopped stalks will compost quickly. The root system will break down, improving drainage and adding organic matter to the top six inches of earth. It's a great solution for breaking up hardpan clay or improving the texture of sandy soil.

Perhaps most practically, barley offers an ornamental quality matched by none. With a strong growing habit, sturdy stalks and spring green-to-golden coloration, barley is a perfect addition to every sunny landscape – it's a beauty queen!

History

I am fascinated with the etymology of words, especially botanical Latin. Most often, the genus and/or species relates to some very useful aspect of the plant: native habitat, function, flower color or foliage attribute. In the case of barley, the name reveals centuries of practicality. The Old English word for barley was "bære," which (due to a linguistic shift of "f" to "b") is similar to the Latin word for flour: farina. In fact, the origins of the word "barn"

translate to "barley house." And further back in history, barley literally fueled the gladiators, who were known as *hordearii* (like the genus name *Horedeum*), aka "barley-eaters"!

Did you know... in the 14th century, King Edward I of England introduced a new measurement system using barley seed? Three barleycorns were equal to one inch. That is where the modern shoe size system originated. My size 7 shoe equals 7 barley seeds long!

Barley was an actual edible commodity used to make soup, bread and beer, meaning when times got tough, you could literally eat your savings! On the downside, it had a very limited shelf life and attracted disease-carrying varmints. Though it may not have been the most practical currency, it was very reliable as a unit of weight.

Barley was one of the first domesticated grains in the Fertile Crescent region, but its early range included North Africa, Crete and the Jordan Valley. The earliest domestication of barley was actually in Tibet. With a native distribution stretching across continents, barley has played a nutritional and economic role in many diverse cultures. Credited as being a key ingredient in the first alcoholic drink in history, barley beer remains the world's third most consumed beverage (after water and tea, *Camellia sinensis*)!

Beer eventually made its way from the Middle East across the Mediterranean and into Europe, where it became an integral part of life.

Fermented barley beer was considered a safe alternative to the often contaminated drinking water of the time. Barley was particularly regarded in the cooler climates of northern Europe, where it thrived in cultivation and provided extensive harvests.

Present Day

Barley remains an important grain for beer, with Russia leading global production. It is also cultivated for the purpose of feeding livestock and is an ingredient in birdseed mixes. For our dinner tables, it is a great whole-grain addition to soups and stews and can be a substitute for rice. When ground into flour, it can be baked into bread that is low in fat and calories, high in fiber and contains antioxidants. But keep in mind, barley flour is not the same as fluffy white wheat flour!

Barley naturally dries over a period of weeks.

Cultural Requirements and Variety Selection

Thriving in temperate climates, barley prefers a temperature range of 25-70°F. Often grown in regions with mild summers, it can be cultivated as a long-day crop, sown in early spring and harvested in late summer. In warmer areas, like where I live in North Carolina, barley is best grown as a cool season, or short-day crop. I sow my barley in late fall and harvest in late spring.

Barley can tolerate a wide range of soil and moisture conditions. However, for ideal growth and development provide well-drained, evenly moist soil and full sun exposure. If you have rich soil, no additional fertilizer will be needed. In lean soil add a balanced fertilizer to ensure proper development through the six-month growing season. Like all plants in the grass family, barley is self-fertile and is wind pollinated. That means it doesn't require pollinators to develop ripe seed.

To understand modern barley you first have to gain an appreciation for where it started and the genetics that evolved over time. Wild barley had a brittle spike that would shatter at maturity and drop its seed. The domestication and breeding of barley has resulted in the development of non-shattering varieties that make mechanized harvesting possible.

Did you know... despite being revered for its beer-making quality, barley flour was considered peasant food throughout Europe? The nobility preferred the flour made from wheat.

In general terms, there are two main categories of barley: two-row and six-row. The most obvious difference between a head of two-row barley and six-row barley is the arrangement of the kernels and the amount of fertile seed that is produced on a spikelet.

- **Two-row barley:** Preferred for beer brewing. Barley grown for brewers malt is called malting barley, as opposed to feed barley.

- **Six-row barley:** Well suited for grinding into flour and using as animal feed. But also used in some beers. Six-row barley is only grown in North America and offers a beautiful seed head with great ornamental qualities.

- **Hulless barley:** "Naked" barley is a form of domesticated barley with an easy-to-remove hull. I recommend 'Sunshine' as a sturdy six-row hulless variety for grinding into flour and because it possesses incredible ornamental qualities.

- **Waxy barley:** Generally, high-protein barley like waxy barley is best suited for animals, including ground-feeding birds like chickens, doves and pheasants. Waxy barley has a lower percentage of amylase and a higher amount of amylopectin, which is easier for poultry to digest. It is recommended that when growing barley for animal feed, especially chickens, you grow a waxy variety because it has higher energy content. There are countless resources online to purchase from and learn more about the specifics for growing your own poultry feed.

Modern varieties have been selected primarily for disease resistance, heat tolerance and structural integrity, aka stem strength. These breeding efforts have improved the plant considerably, especially for mechanized harvests. As a novice home grower harvesting by hand, I remain impressed with the common varieties I have ordered from online seed sources. Just Google "barley seed" and you will find a wide assortment of very affordable seed. *Good to know:* as of now, there are no genetically modified barley varieties for sale or in commercial production in North America.

Final Thoughts

I don't want to imagine a world without barley, because I enjoy a cold beer after a hot day in the garden! Beyond that obvious fact, my experience as a gardener has been enhanced greatly with the addition of barley in my home landscape. It is a great conversation starter, as well as a muse for my inner photographer. The biomass and roots help improve my soil and the seeds provide food for passing birds. Though I may not be cultivating barley in the traditional agronomic way, it plays an important role within the boundaries of my suburban landscape.

That's the privilege of being a gardener in the current age: We can cultivate plants just for beauty or curiosity – for the pleasure of it. But of course, there was a time, not so long ago, when that was not the case. And though barley is, without a doubt, the most beautiful plant I have ever laid eyes on, it offers this world so much more.

These Jr Master Gardeners harvested barley for the first time.

Oats – The Dancer
Avena sativa

Oats

Introduction

It was another light bulb moment for me the day I came across oat seed and actually appreciated what it was. Of course I had grown up eating oatmeal and must have seen fields of oats as a child in the Midwest, but it wasn't until a chance encounter with a bag of seed that I put it all together.

Thanks to Fifth Season Gardening, who stocked 1-pound bags of oat seed (likely intended for hungry backyard chickens), my oat growing adventure began. Though I have never grown enough oats for eating, at least not yet, they are a valuable addition to my late spring garden with their tall four-foot stature and wide blades of silver-blue foliage. As a cool season grass it is a standout, and when the delicate seed heads appear they will captivate your imagination. Seeming to dance in the breeze, oats offer a less formal structure and can be seamlessly woven into perennial and shrub borders.

After a few years of growing grains, I have noticed a few key things, one being that oats are more frost sensitive compared to the other cool season cereals I cultivate. This observation has been consistent each winter, as the tender shoots that germinate in December can burn to the ground with the first night in the upper teens. Initially I thought they were a lost cause, but happily, the oats persevered and thrived once spring-like temperatures arrived. Yet, every January I have a moment when I question if those oat clumps will rebound. Trust me, they will.

Oats are particularly valuable as a scavenger, considering the roots stretch throughout the top 36 inches of ground. These deep roots draw important nutrients up to the soil surface, ultimately providing high rates of available nutrients and microorganism activity that will benefit future crops.

They are also an important plant in crop rotations. Most commonly paired with peas, a legume that will naturally fix nitrogen in the soil, oats are grown not only for their edible whole-grain seed, but for their hay and overall organic matter, the green mulch. When cultivated and turned back into the ground they help improve the soil structure, drainage and aeration, thus setting up the next planting for success.

HARD-PACKED SOIL? OATS TO THE RESCUE!

Do you live in a newly-built home with difficult soil? Good news: Oats can be used as an efficient tool to quickly improve hard-packed earth, especially in new developments where so many home gardeners struggle to establish plantings. One season of growing oats will alleviate many of the difficulties created by heavy equipment used for clearing land. Consider the fibrous roots of oats to be the ultimate Rototiller. Their roots do all the work, so you can garden smart, not hard.

Field-grown oats in Lancaster, Pennsylvania.

I didn't know any of this the first time I sowed oats. I was just a curious gardener with an appetite for growing something new to me. The cost-effective seed, ease of germination and growth habit quickly made oats a "can't live without" cool season grain in my home garden. I bet you will agree once you give it a try!

History

It amuses me to learn about how food crops have defined societal hierarchy over the centuries. Oats are no exception. For instance, in Samuel Johnson's 1755 *Dictionary of the English Language*, oats were defined as "eaten by people in Scotland, but fit only for horses in England." To which many a Scot has been known to reply, "That's why England has such good horses and Scotland such fine men." In the past, many cultures dismissed the vast nutritional attributes of oats.

Did you know... it wasn't until the 1980s that oats were recognized as healthy food by nutritionists? Today, you will be hard-pressed to find a granola bar without oats in the list of ingredients.

Oats have a long, storied history, despite being considered the last of the cereal grains to be cultivated. The modern oat as we know it was likely derived from the Asian wild red oat about 3,000 years ago. Considered a secondary cereal crop, oats were less favored due to their lack of flavor and short shelf life. In fact, the Greeks and Romans thought of oats to be "diseased wheat, only suitable for animals."

Of course oats were very important for the cultivation of animals, providing greens to graze upon and soft, dust-free straw to bed in. Animals weren't the only creatures that relied on the dried stalks of oats for slumber. For centuries, people made beds from oat straw to seek comfort from the chill of the hard ground.

The one big advantage of oats, as compared to other cereal grains, is their tolerance of cold, wet climates. Their ability to thrive in difficult environments is why oats spread quickly throughout Asia and Europe, to become a mainstay crop to this day in countries like Ireland, Scotland and Iceland.

From the beginning, oats have been grown for medicinal purposes. (It is now known that oats help stabilize blood sugar and enhance immune systems, and that eating whole oats can offer protection against cardiovascular disease.) Oats have been used in cosmetics and cleansing products for over a thousand years. Like other grains, oats were also malted for alcohol production, namely oatmeal stout beers.

But oats were most commonly grown as animal fodder. Fields were sown for fresh grazing and the leaves were harvested to provide edible straw for the off season. Every aspect of the oat plant is useful: roots, stem, leaves and seed. To that point, oats have been an important agricultural tool not just as a crop, but as a means of improving compacted soil, increasing fertility and providing a layer of organic matter in over-farmed land. This green fertilizer method of turning the crop under is of particular importance in healing damaged land and has been utilized for many centuries.

Oats grow well with cool season companions like poppies and larkspur.

Present Day

Today's oats are grown commercially both for human and animal consumption. The leaves are harvested fresh for grazing and dried as straw and are of particular importance in commercial agricultural production.

Besides their medicinal benefits, mentioned above, oats have an important use in modern cosmetics and skin cleansers, as they contain a natural soothing protein that can relieve troubled skin. (Fun fact: Aveena takes its name from the botanical name for oats, *Avena sativa*, because all of its products are based on oats.) And it was Cheerios, the standard breakfast of my childhood, that by clever advertising helped raise awareness of the nutritional benefits of whole-grain oats. The accessibility of brands such as Quaker and their invention of instant oats secured their role as a mainstay in diets across the world.

Cultural Requirements and Variety Selection

Best grown in temperate regions, oats have a lower summer heat requirement and tolerate more rain than other cereals. This trait is why they were embraced in regions with cool, wet summers in northwest Europe. They also perform quite well in northern regions of the United States and Canada, as a spring-sown fall-harvested crop. For those of us gardening in warmer climates, oats are an excellent winter-active plant, being sown in late fall and harvested in late spring. They perform best in full sun with evenly moist soil, and do not require excessive soil fertility. In my early days of growing oats I added organic fertilizer and irrigated, both of which were totally unnecessary for my in-ground crops. As a container specimen, additional fertilizer and water may be needed.

Because oats are quick to germinate and establish, they are also effective at choking out their competition, aka weeds. And with few pests and diseases, they rank in my top 1% of lowest maintenance plants I've ever grown. Some years, my crops may show signs of rust mid-season, and though unsightly, it does not seem to have a major impact on the overall development of the plant or seed. As with powdery mildew, I just accept rust as one of the realities I face as a gardener. In my experience of growing novel crops, leaf rust is not cause for alarm.

HULLESS OATS: The first variety I grew was labeled "hulless," which technically refers to *Avena nuda,* a different species. The advantage of growing a hulless oat is for ease of home processing. So if you are growing oats with the intention of making your own oatmeal, I highly recommend cultivating a hulless selection such as 'Streaker', which can be found through online seed sources. When harvested and threshed, the hulless oat kernels shed most of the inedible hulls that persist on common oats.

Once I realized how complicated grain nomenclature was, I started sleuthing around online to discover a ton of information about oat varieties, most of which did not relate to my needs. Here's the bottom line: As a beginner, just stick to growing varieties that are easy to

The wide, silver-blue foliage of oats add a dynamic ornamental appeal.

find from your usual seed sources. I buy my seed from Baker Creek Heirloom Seed, Johnny's Seed and my local shop, Fifth Season Gardening. Retail sources often choose the varieties that are easiest for home gardeners to grow.

Final Thoughts

Considering my favorite beer of all time is Guinness, an oatmeal stout, I have a deep appreciation for the flavor oats provide. They are an important source of fiber – most granola and energy bars include oats, after all. But besides their nutritional value, oats are a grain with a delicate beauty like no other and deserve consideration as a landscape plant. The wide, silver-blue blades of foliage add dynamic contrast and the dancing seed heads provide interest that few other grasses offer. With low maintenance needs, it is hard not to recommend a few clumps of cleverly placed oats in every landscape, if only to add an element of amusement, education and seasonal intrigue.

Wheat – The Workhorse
Triticum aestivum

Wheat

Introduction

Wheat was my introduction to growing grains. It captured my heart and attention from the start. The moment I scattered the seed my life as a a gardener (and a consumer of carbohydrates) changed forever. My first "suburban grain experiment" was an eye-opening experience on many levels, from discovering the beauty of grains to developing an appreciation for the modern advances of breeding. Wheat is a crop that seems to have endless potential and purpose in common landscape applications.

I have had a lot of funny moments since I became a grain grower. One of the first things I realized upon growing grains was the importance of clear enunciation. I recall declaring in front of an auditorium of gardeners that I was growing wheat, to which I heard loud gasps. "Not weed!" I quickly clarified, "Wheat...like where bread comes from." That explanation has stuck, and now every school grain installation is called a bread garden so no one will be confused!

Considering I had no expectations when I started growing wheat, the journey has been particularly joyful. Admittedly, growing wheat is the easy part. In reality, most people are not going to go through the trouble of hand harvesting, threshing and milling wheat into flour. Sometimes, growing a plant can simply be for the joy of experimentation. In my case, after two seasons of grinding my own flour, I now grow wheat to enjoy as an ornamental element that also improves my native garden soil. Only small amounts are processed for cooking, as the birds also compete for my ripe seed.

A WORD ABOUT SOIL: Soil improvement has become the most practical driving force behind my devotion to cultivating wheat. During the growing season, the deep roots will absorb nitrogen that has leached through the soil profile, and they will move these nutrients toward the surface.

IN THE LANDSCAPE: As a landscape plant, wheat checks all of the value boxes. First, it is a very inexpensive investment – you can buy a pound of seed for under five dollars. It is also one of the lowest maintenance crops that you will ever grow. Once you have sown it you leave it alone until the stalks dry six months later. It provides color, texture, insect habitat and birdseed. When it turns amber and the light shines through, you will become addicted to its beauty, as I have. The dried stalks are perfect for flower arrangements and holiday decorations and provide ample reason to grow a few clumps and not even think about traditional harvest practices.

History

Believe it or not, wheat would not have survived in the wild as it was 10,000 years ago. In the big-picture web of life on planet Earth, wheat shines as an example of the role human beings have played in the successful evolution of plants over thousands of years with careful cultivation and selection improvements.

Wheat was one of the first grains to be domesticated in the Fertile Crescent approximately 11,000 years ago. In fact, the domestication of wheat marks the Neolithic timeframe. This era is identified by the domestication of crops and animals, ultimately leading to the development of community, farming and the invention of metal tools.

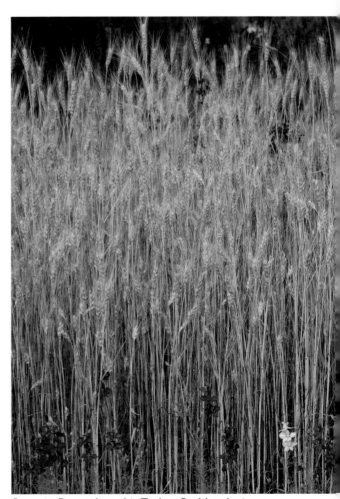

Sown in December, this Turkey Red hard winter wheat dries alongside colorful larkspur in mid-June in my North Carolina garden.

Field-grown wheat is ready for combine harvesting.

Did you know... wheat only really became a commodity after the mid–1800s? It was as a result of machine creation.

Mechanized reaping and threshing allowed farmers to greatly increase productivity. Advancements in steam engines and the internal combustion engine in the late 1800s and early 1900s completely transformed the planting and harvesting process. Yet again, without continuous human ingenuity, wheat would not have evolved to its current status.

Present Day

I often think of how challenging it would be to feed the current world's population if we hadn't harnessed the power of cereal grains, namely wheat. Global trade of wheat is greater than all other crops combined. Since 1960, world production of wheat has tripled and is expected to continue to grow throughout the 21st century. Societies across the globe depend on wheat for fundamental sources of nutrients.

Today in America, we seem to be in a love-hate relationship with carbohydrate sources. There is much to be discovered regarding the causes of celiac disease and other gluten intolerances and sensitivities. Consumer concerns about GMOs and persistent herbicide applications are at an all-time high and are not entirely unjust. I find there are more questions than definitive answers, which is why growing your own grains can be a beneficial experience.

As with all the grains, the next several thousand years proved to be important as cultivation spread across Europe and Asia. By 4,000 B.C., bread wheat had become a staple food for European, Middle Eastern and Western Asian cultures.

It wasn't until the 1500s that wheat was introduced to the Western Hemisphere, courtesy of the Spaniards who first brought it to Mexico. Over the next 250 years American settlers brought varieties from northern Europe that thrived in the colonies and ultimately cultivated "the wheat belt."

At the very least, you know how the crop was grown and the gluten/protein level of the cultivar you are growing, since levels vary greatly by variety.

It is because of my experience growing wheat in my home garden that I have become more open-minded and knowledgeable about the importance of modern plant breeding and the science of genetic modifications for long-term crop improvements and sustainable growing practices.

Cultural Requirements and Variety Selection

One of the greatest attributes of wheat is how well adapted it is in a variety of climates. Wheat is a winter crop in my Zone 7 climate, but can be grown through the summer in northern gardens. It is easily grown from seed and there are many varieties, both modern and ancient, to choose from. In my experience, modern cultivars boast improvements in disease resistance and structural integrity, making them better garden specimens. I recommend growing a few varieties of each so you can compare the difference in your region.

Wheat seed will germinate readily, either in the ground directly or in communal flats or pots to transplant as clumps. Sow in well-drained, moist, organic soil in full sun. Add an organic fertilizer at the time of sowing, especially in poor soils. This will provide all the nutrients for the six to seven-month growing season and ensure your plants are productive. Germination will occur within 14 days and the bright green

'Black Eagle' wheat has dark awns and dries well for arrangements.

new growth will look just like grass – because wheat is a grass in the *Poacaceae* family!

As you can imagine, over the course of 10,000 years many hybrids of *Triticum* were created, which is why I find the nomenclature of wheat to be the most confusing of any plant. Perhaps this is one example of common names reigning supreme.

There are several types of wheat to choose from with regard to their culinary use:

- **Soft wheat** varieties have starchy kernels with less gluten and are preferred for biscuits, piecrust, French bread and much more.
- **Hard wheat** has higher protein and gluten levels and is milled into flour suitable for bread and cake.
- **Durham** is the hardest wheat seed and its flour is used to make pasta.

(More about culinary uses on the next pages.)

WHAT ABOUT A VARIETY'S GENETIC PROFILE?

Another variety consideration relates to the genetic profile. It gets a bit complicated, as some species are diploids, meaning they have only two sets of chromosomes. Others are polyploids, with either four or six sets of chromosomes. Before I lose you, let me explain further: The ancient strain of einkorn wheat is a diploid (only two sets of chromosomes), whereas emmer and durum wheat are tetraploid, with four sets of chromosomes. Common bread wheat and spelt selections have six sets of chromosomes known as hexaploids. Still there?

This information may seem unnecessary to the average home gardener, but it is important to recognize the genetic differences between the varieties because these play a role in their performance.

WHY I'M A FAN OF POLYPLOID WHEAT: In my experience, I find the polyploid selections to have better structural integrity, higher yields and more biomass to compost back into the soil. Whereas diploid wheat lacks stem strength and is prone to lodging, particularly in wind storms when the seed is reaching maturity and the weight exceeds the strength of the stem. Lodging, where the stalk bends or breaks close to the ground, is a major problem with all cereal grains, especially "Old World" wheat.

Generally, wheat cultivars are classified by several characteristics, including planting season, color and hardness of the grain. For example, winter wheat is ideal for growers in climates with mild winter temperatures, like mine. In contrast, spring wheat is best suited for northern gardeners who experience a temperate summer climate. As a gardener in the Southeast United States, I exclusively grow winter wheat.

SOFT WHEAT: Soft wheat is categorized by color: red or white.

- **Soft red** wheat has low protein content and is used to make pastries including cookies, cakes and donuts.

Stem strength is an important consideration.

- **Soft white** provides a whiter product for high quality crackers and Asian-style noodles, as well as many bakery products other than bread. It also is a high-yielding variety with excellent performance in the home landscape.

HARD WHEAT: Hard wheat is broken into three main distinctions: red, white and durum.

- **Hard red** wheat accounts for than 40% of the U.S. wheat crop and half of American wheat exports. It has high levels of protein and is primarily used for breads and all-purpose flour.
- **Hard white** wheat offers a sweeter flavor and is used in yeast breads, hard rolls, tortillas and whole wheat and all-purpose flour. It is also used in brewing beer.
- **Durum**, a spring wheat, is the hardest grain variety and is primarily used to make pasta, as mentioned above. It can be found in both red and white selections.

Final Thoughts

I encourage everyone I meet to consider planting wheat seed at least once in their life. It is a unique garden experience, one worth noting. For me, after one season of growing wheat I developed a deep appreciation for what farmers provide us. Considering how durable, inexpensive and low maintenance wheat is, it certainly deserves more attention in today's home landscape realm. From mixed meadows to sleek clumps mimicking typical ornamental grass plantings, the design opportunities are limitless. ∎

Six

Three Great Warm Season Grains
Corn • Rice • Sorghum

*H*eat loving grains offer a lot of visual appeal in addition to their abundant harvests. Corn, rice and sorghum all thrive in the summer heat and grow best in full sun, just like their cool season counterparts. Since these crops are frost sensitive and need warm soil (temperatures over 55°F), they are best planted a few weeks after your last frost date. If you live in a northern region, these should be started indoors and transplanted, to ensure they will develop to their fullest potential.

Each warm season grain has its own unique attributes and can provide solutions for common landscape problems. From soil improvement to absorbing excess water, these crops are beautiful and practical. If you have never grown them, it is well worth the small investment in seed to see for yourself!

Colorful corn and millet can be harvested and used for autumn decorations.

Corn – The Catalyst for Change
Zea mays

Corn

Introduction

In my Midwest childhood years, seeing corn meant summer had arrived. "Knee-high by the Fourth of July" was a true indication of the season. And fresh corn on the cob meant the county 4-H fair was not far away. The endless fields that stretched to the horizons surrounded me, and like most people, I took that scene for granted. It seemed this crop grew bountifully with no effort at all.

The term "maize" is actually preferred in scientific and international usage. Like most common names, the term "corn" has a complex variety of meanings that vary regionally. You can consider corn to be a secondary descriptive word for a specific attribute of maize – think sweet corn, corn on the cob, baby corn, popcorn or corn flakes. But for the purposes of this book, I am sticking with the name I know, corn, a crop with many uses.

GROWING CORN IS SO EASY: It grows in warm climates everywhere. You plant the seed in the ground and they will germinate. With its high threshold for drought, you don't have to be a seasoned grower to get corn to yield. So why don't more home gardeners grow it?

I ponder that question all the time, about corn and all the cereals that are featured in this book. Perhaps it is their association with row crop agriculture that has all but taken them out of consideration by home gardeners. That is unfortunate, since our diets revolve around these plants that are so conspicuously absent from our home growing environments. Clearly, we live in a time where people are far removed from their food sources and have little to no daily reminders about the food chain – or the concept of becoming an active participant in it.

Or, it could simply be a space and time dynamic. I'm here to banish the assumption that you have to grow a large plot that will take a lot of time to harvest, process and preserve. This is true if you are growing acres, but most home gardeners (like me) who live in the suburbs, do not have that kind of space. Instead, consider growing a dozen plants and space them a few feet apart throughout your landscape. This way you can enjoy a small harvest that won't consume all your free time!

I FIND BEAUTY IN A CORN STALK: Some might say that corn lacks the "beauty" of ornamental plants and can become messy as they dry. I used to think that, too, because I was accustomed to seeing corn as a field crop. The dried stalks remind me of fall decorations, but I don't want that look in my home landscape. One year, I sowed a few clumps as an experiment and gave myself permission to cut them down the moment they looked untidy. My opinion of corn was transformed as I watched the bright green leaves unfurl and the strong stalks rise to the sky. When the tassels waved in the breeze the scent reminded me of the summers from my childhood. Now today, harvesting the fresh ears from my own front yard and sharing the harvests with family and friends has given me a new perspective on the possibilities an ordinary landscape offers.

Those are the insights of a home gardener, and it is my sincere hope these words will inspire you to grow more food, especially crops that are easy and practical while offering dynamic architectural interest. Corn is a plant that every summer gardener should include, if for no other reason than to have a few exclamation points dotted throughout your design. The bonus is harvesting the delicious ears, both fresh and dried. That is something you will never get from your typical ornamental grass.

Beautiful corn foliage adds color and texture to the landscape.

History

Corn is a cereal grain first domesticated in southern Mexico about 10,000 years ago. There is some debate about how it hybridized and eventually spread across Central, North and South America: Was it by multiple independent domestications or a single domestication of the plant? Either way, corn is another example of a cereal that co-evolved with humans. It is thought that corn would not even exist today if it weren't for the hybridizations and selections that people made thousands of years ago. Yes, long before GMO was a cause for concern, people were modifying their maize.

After the arrival of Europeans in 1492, Spanish settlers began to eat corn, though it was not the staple cereal of their choosing. They preferred wheat bread to New World foods such as corn, cassava and potatoes – believing these native foods lacked nutrition and would be weakening. Of course necessity won out, and there is archeological evidence that Spanish settlers not only ate corn, they grew it.

Explorers and traders (Spanish and Portuguese) carried it back to Europe and it spread to the rest of the world because of its ability to grow in diverse climates. Just a few decades after Columbus' voyage to the New World, corn was cultivated in Spain, and then in Portugal, Italy and into Africa.

Present Day

Maize remains the most widely grown crop in the world, with total production surpassing that of wheat or rice. However, very little of this is consumed directly by humans; most is used for corn ethanol, animal feed and other products such as corn starch and corn syrup, common additives in processed food.

With 14.6 billion bushels produced in the United States in 2018, it ranks as the #1 crop grown throughout the Americas. Approximately 40% of that harvest is used for corn ethanol, which is derived from corn biomass and processed through fermentation and distillation.

Did you know... corn is the main source for ethanol fuel in the United States? It is fair to say if you drive a car you have purchased corn-based ethanol.

In recent years, corn has caused a lot of controversy. The USDA estimates that 90% of the corn grown in the United States in 2018 was a GMO or herbicide-tolerant variety. The vast majority of that was used as animal feed and for making ethanol, but the concern remains the same. With Roundup Ready seed and other genetic modifications a reality of our time, there is a lot to learn about the new era of corn and what the future will hold for this economic driver.

THE MORE YOU KNOW... Corn is an important aspect of the North American economy. From university researchers to biotech giants and small family farmers, corn is a staple in traditional agriculture and will continue to evolve, for better or worse. Since I still have more questions than answers about what all of this means, my best advice is to do your part in educating yourself, support local farmers whose growing ethic aligns with yours and try your hand at cultivating corn at home. When you change a few habits at the grocery store you can effect meaningful change.

Too often, the general public takes a complex issue and goes right to a simplified version of "right or wrong." Loud media sound bites can drive opinions, but that is not how solutions are created. Instead, we should all be actively engaged in intelligent conversations regarding the reality of current conventional agriculture, which is responsible for feeding a growing global population at a time when food prices are lower than ever.

WHAT'LL YOU HAVE?

Consumable alcohol is another place you can find corn in your life. Have you ever enjoyed a sip of bourbon whiskey? Then you have indulged in corn-based liquor. Considered "America's Native Spirit," bourbon first started to appear in the late 18th century in Kentucky. As a home corn grower, I have never made my own bourbon, but knowing that I could if times got really tough provides me endless entertainment!

Other corn-based spirits include the popular Tito's Vodka brand, my favorite vodka. It has a sweeter flavor compared to the traditional formulations made from grains like wheat or rice, or tubers such as potato. Everclear is another corn-based spirit, one that has a very high alcohol volume of 95%! In recent years, "corn whiskey" has been marketed and sold as legal moonshine, with a distinguishing characteristic of being un-aged and with a maximum strength of 80%.

Corn is the only cereal grain native to the Western Hemisphere and it plays an important role in our daily lives. The concept of "everything in moderation" should apply not only to the consumption of corn in all its different forms, but also to our assumptions about conventional agriculture and food science. The more we know, the better we will be!

Grow corn for use as an ornamental plant as well as for its garden bounty.

Cultural Requirements and Variety Selection

Corn will thrive in a sunny location through the heat of the summer in most environments. Though it will tolerate poor soils, you will have healthier plants with higher yields if you incorporate organic matter into your soil and supplement water during extreme heat and dryness. I recommend adding a soaker hose or setting a sprinkler up on a timer so the plants never get drought-stressed.

Corn in your garden

Here are some important considerations when growing corn at home – especially as a landscape element, instead of the traditional rows:

SPACING: You need to plant corn close to one another to ensure that proper pollination occurs. Like all grass plants, corn is wind-pollinated, meaning the pollen is blown from the male tassels and falls onto the female silks. Close proximity of the stalks will enhance the pollination rate, resulting in full cobs for your enjoyment.

SOIL TEMPERATURE: I live in a region where this is not an issue. But I do recall seeing people go to great lengths in the North to get their corn beds prepared. Spreading black plastic over the area where you plan to grow is a great way to heat the soil and extend your growing season, as many varieties will need at least three months from sowing to mature harvest. Mounds or raised beds can also be helpful to increase your soil temperatures earlier in the season. Many cultivars require soil temperatures of at least 65°F for proper germination and root development. That is usually two to three weeks after your last frost date. Always check with a local extension agent about the best practices for your area.

NITROGEN: Corn loves nitrogen, so be prepared to add a nitrogen-rich fertilizer when you plant. In addition to aged compost as a soil amendment, cottonseed meal and feather meal are great sources of nitrogen (N). Dust the surface at a rate of three pounds per 100 square feet, or as I do it: one handful per seed. I also recommend watering a few times a season with fish emulsion to guarantee the plants will stay bright green and look fresh.

PESTS AND DISEASES: Not to discourage you, but in years past I have had corn earworms come through and devour every single kernel. But fear not, there are a few easy-to-apply methods that will help with this:

- When the plants first germinate, cover with a small screen or piece of row cover to exclude birds, caterpillars and beetles from the start.

- You can dust plants with BT (*Bacillus thurigensis*) to eliminate caterpillars as the plants mature.

- To deter earworms, simply apply five drops of vegetable oil to the silks of each ear.

- My best recommendation for disease control is to select varieties that have resistance and keep your plants growing in the best conditions possible.

Corn earworms left untreated can damage the cob.

ONE MORE THING: Uneven moisture can lead to decline, so make sure you keep your corn watered evenly and you will reduce trouble.

HARVEST TIME: Knowing when to harvest your sweet corn can be confusing, especially for beginning growers. The general rule is to begin harvesting ears three weeks after the first silks appear. When the silks turn brown, check the ears to make sure the kernels are fully developed. You can also squeeze a kernel with your fingernail: If white milky juice drips out, that is the sign that the ear is ripe and ready for picking.

NOTE: Harvesting popcorn or ornamental varieties is different: You are going to leave them all on the stalk until the entire plant dries out.

Did you know... there are more than 250 different subspecies of maize around the world?

'Earth Tones' dent corn is a new favorite for decorating and grinding when it is dried.

There are five major types of corn grown agriculturally: dent, flint, flour, popcorn and sweet corn. Sugar-rich varieties of sweet corn are usually grown for fresh eating, while field corn varieties serve as a source of animal feed and ethanol, in addition to being ground into cornmeal or masa and pressed into corn oil for human consumption. And...once fermentated and distilled, field corn is transformed into bourbon whiskey!

There are no GMO corn varieties available to the home grower, so no need for concern. However, corn is open-pollinated; meaning the pollen from one plant can easily blow onto another, contaminating future seed. This makes it difficult to ensure that your non-GMO corn will not be cross-pollinated by a commercial variety, especially if you live near a farm where conventional corn is grown. For this reason I recommend you purchase your corn seed from a certified source each year. (See Resources, page 187, for a listing of trusted seed companies.)

Sweet corn for fresh eating

Most home gardeners want to grow sweet corn for fresh eating. It is the taste of summer, after all. Flavor and adaptability to your climate are the main considerations when choosing a variety. There are three main types of fresh-eating sweet corn, which are classified by flavor:

- standard
- sugary enhanced
- super sweet

Always consult with a local professional to learn which varieties are best for growing in your area.

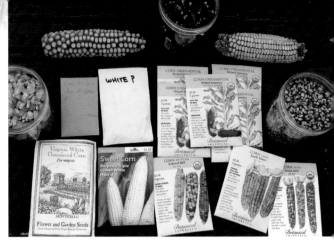

Here are some of the sources I use for the corn varieties that I grow.

STANDARD corn is considered the "old-fashioned," heirloom or open-pollinated type of corn that was the standard for generations past. It will tolerate being planted in cool soil, down to around 55°F, and is best eaten immediately after harvest. There are a number of good cultivars in this category including 'Butter and Sugar', 'Jubilee', and my favorite, 'Silver Queen'. With its sweet white kernels and large ears, 'Silver Queen' is well adapted to many climates and the ears hold up well after harvest, which is why this is commonly available at markets and farm stands.

SUGARY ENHANCED corn varieties are hybrids that keep their flavor longer once they have been harvested. This is extremely important for commercial growers, who have to monitor the crops to harvest at peak sweetness. These selections do not require daily evaluation, saving the farmer precious hours during a busy season. One big difference with sugary enhanced varieties is their need

Harvested sweet corn

for soil temperatures to be at least 65°F for germination. This means they have to be sown later or be grown in milder regions where soil warms earlier. Consider growing varieties such as 'Breeders Choice' and 'Kandy Korn', and a wonderful All-American Selections (AAS) choice known as 'How Sweet It Is'. I am partial to AAS varieties because they have gone through vigorous trialing across the United States to test overall performance, yield, flavor and disease resistance. This variety checks off all my must-have boxes, which is why I grow it every single summer. It is a slightly shorter variety, growing to just over six feet tall and is widely adapted to climates in North America.

SUPER SWEET corn varieties are also hybrids, considered the sweetest of all in the marketplace. They require a bit more maintenance compared to sugary enhanced varieties, with a shelf life of only a few days post-harvest. They are also very sensitive to cold and require soil temperatures to be at least up to 65°F for germination. In northern regions where temperatures are mild, you can pre-germinate seedlings in pots and then transplant them into your garden once the warm days of real summer arrive. 'Butterfruit Original Early' is a great variety that matures in about 70 days. It has bright yellow kernels and tightly packed ears. What I love about this cultivar is how short the plant is. Growing to only five feet tall, this offers a lot of versatility in the landscape while having good disease resistance. Other varieties of note include 'Early Xtra Sweet', another AAS winner, and 'Sweetie', which holds its flavor longer both on the stalk and post-harvest. The stalks will grow to six feet tall and it reaches maturity in 85 days. It is an excellent choice for home growers and has 30% fewer calories than regular corn!

OTHER TYPES OF CORN suitable for home growers include baby corn, dent corn, popcorn and ornamental varieties. I love growing these "untraditional" selections because I am often travelling when my sweet corn is ready to be harvested.

Baby corn

I grew 'Baby Asian' for the first time a few years ago because one of the things I always order at a Chinese restaurant is baby corn. The finger-sized cobs have tender white kernels and are perfect for stir-fries and pickling. To be honest, I was so enamored that I ate most them as soon as I picked them, and sadly didn't capture any images of my harvest because I was too busy gobbling them up. I forgot to buy seed last year but have just sown 25 plants, so I look forward to enjoying my baby corn again this season.

Popcorn!

Popcorn is another staple in my home garden and every single school garden I visit, because who doesn't like popcorn? If you want to get the next generation excited about growing, start with popcorn! It is important to note that popcorn has a longer growing requirement, averaging 100 days from planting to harvesting. Here in my Zone 7 region, growing popcorn to maturity is not a problem, as we have nearly seven frost-free months. In northern areas you may need to pre-germinate your popcorn and transplant when your soil temperatures are warm enough.

Like sweet corn, popcorn wants to grow in full sun and evenly moist soil with extra nitrogen. All of these popcorn varieties will grow about seven feet tall and are therefore best suited for mid-to-back borders and can be used as a seasonal screen. You harvest popcorn when the plant is completely dried, so you don't need to check the ears mid-season, but if you find you have an earworm or caterpillar problem, follow the instructions on page 79 to ensure your cobs will be perfectly formed and ready for popping.

CHOOSE YOUR COLOR: There are a ton of popcorn varieties in the market, but I like to keep it simple and grow by color. Black, gold and white cover the spectrum and when mixed together look really pretty in a jar.

Black popcorn – large and flavorful

- Black popcorn has deep-blue kernels that pop white and have a rich flavor. The main difference between this variety and standard popcorn is the ear size: Black popcorn ears are larger, up to about eight inches long.

- Gold popcorn is an excellent popping corn with large puffed kernels and ears that range from six to eight inches long.

- 'White Cloud' is my preferred white kernel popcorn. It has small, plump ears only four inches long. Despite the small ear size, it is a high-yielding variety and does very well in regions with cooler temperatures.

'Glass Gem' is a beautiful variety.

Ornamental varieties

Corn comes in a wide range of ornamental varieties, commonly displayed on Thanksgiving tables with vibrant colored kernels. This doesn't mean they can't be eaten. Consider the Virginia heirloom variety of dent corn called 'Bloody Butcher'. With dark red kernels, this plant is an edible ornamental and a staple for me, both in the garden and in the kitchen, as I love to grind it into grits.

Like popcorn, these varieties grow through the summer and are harvested when the entire plant has dried out. The average time from seeding to harvesting is around 100 days in all climates: June through October.

- 'Glass Gem' is a new introduction that has been widely heralded as the most beautiful corn ever grown. I agree. This variety was bred from a number of native selections by the famous Cherokee corn collector Carl "White Eagle" Barnes. The coloration is pastel with many shades of lavender-purple, pink, blue and yellow. Truly a sight to be seen. Every home gardener should try this at least one time in your life. I would never consider my garden complete without it.

- 'Indian Corn' is aptly named for its decorative ears boasting kernels of blue, red, purple, orange and white.

- 'Rainbow' is another multi-colored variety, also commonly referred to as "Indian corn." The large, smooth ears are attractive for fall decorating, but you can harvest this variety when young and roast it for eating.

Final Thoughts

Since corn has become the poster child for much that is wrong with modern scientific advancements in food production, it seems appropriate to encourage you to grow more of it yourself, in your own soil, on your own terms. It is a beautiful, productive native plant.

Most of all, I want you to enjoy the beauty and bounty of corn, instead of focusing on all the possible negatives. I find that when I grow a plant my appreciation deepens, not only for the plant itself, but for the industry that supports its development. So give corn a try! At the very least you will have some homegrown Halloween-Thanksgiving decorations to use.

Rice – The Mystifier
Oryza sativa

Rice

Rice is grown in paddies that are flooded for one specific purpose: weed suppression. Unaffected by flooding, the rice plant thrives while its competitors drown. The water serves as a natural form of herbicide. However, growing in water is not required, which is what makes rice such an ideal plant for home gardens. It will thrive in the same conditions as many of our best-loved summer annuals, including begonias, coleus and sweet potato vine.

With recent record-breaking rainfall in much of North America, growing plants that are more tolerant of wet feet is on the minds of many gardeners, including myself. As we all seek solutions to shed excess water from our properties, the answer is simple: Plant water-loving things like rice! This may be exactly what you need to help absorb heavy rainfall while creating an ornamental feature in your landscape.

Did you know... rice is unique in that it is the one grain that is very tolerant of saturation?

You can grow rice in any sunny area with supplemental irrigation. I grow it in many different locations, from my foundation landscape to a variety of different containers.

Introduction

When I tell people I grow rice, I am always met with looks of mystification. Most people have never seen a rice plant growing. It is a staple food crop eaten around the globe, yet it's never in my lifetime been considered a home gardening plant. That is probably due to the general assumption that rice has to grow in water.

Rice has thrived as a beautiful feature every way I have cultivated it and is an instant conversation starter. Visitors never seem to be able to identify the random grass that is planted around my garden and when they learn what it is they are totally captivated, confused and eager to learn more!

MY FIRST ENCOUNTER WITH RICE GROWING IN A GARDEN: Rice wasn't a crop I would have ever considered if it weren't for my dear friend and local gardener Som Dewey Sibharath. During a visit to his suburban Holly Springs, N.C., garden, I was introduced for the first time to the rice plant. Cultivating rice was part of his gardening heritage, having grown up in Laos – and a move to the United States didn't need to change that.

There, in Dewey's USDA Zone 7b garden, the bright green blades of rice foliage shone in the sunlight. With temperatures already in the low 90s, instead of wilting in the heat, his rice plants stretched robustly while their roots were busy absorbing all the extra moisture from an overnight thunderstorm.

Dewey cultivated his rice the traditional way, by transplanting small clumps of germinated seed into beds that can be flooded. His simple, genius set-up ensured healthy plants with high yields and no weed competition. It looked just like any other boxed bed, but here he was, cultivating a crop that most home gardeners have never even seen. I left his house that day with a pot full of rice seedlings and a new perspective.

Naturally, I was excited and curious about cultivating this plant that I have eaten my entire life but had never seen growing. Even during my visits to Charleston, S.C., where rice had once been a "crop of gold," I had never knowingly seen rice in cultivation. So many questions filled my head, namely, where should I plant Dewey's gift and how can I get my hands on more?

A quick Google search revealed a few hundred sources, including my go-to, Baker Creek Heirloom Seed. My orders were placed immediately and within two weeks of that first introduction in Dewey's back yard, my journey as a rice grower began.

Like the other grains detailed in this book, I started growing rice out of curiosity. I had no intention of growing it for consumption. Coming from the ornamental plant industry, I first see a plant's value as decorative or as solving some cultural problem in a landscape. Cultivation for the purpose of harvest is often a secondary consideration for me, as I strive to design and manage gardens that are first beautiful and inspiring, before productive and farm-like. In the case of rice, it was an opportunity to test the limits of a new-to-me plant. Regardless of the outcome, growing rice would offer an authentic experience and a lot of Instagram photos for the season.

Som Dewey Sibharath and his mother. Those beautiful rice beds are part of his Laotian gardening heritage.

Rice is perfect for growing in containers.

After researching online, I set out to grow this crop in a different way, one that other home gardeners could relate to. No miniature paddies, but instead, creative and thoughtful placement to take advantage of excess moisture.

RICE IN CONTAINERS: Rice is the best grain to grow in a container. It is very well suited for daily watering and thrives in a sunny location. This was my initial approach to growing those rice seedlings Dewey shared with me, and they were a great success all summer long. I grow in both traditional pots with drainage holes and in solid vessels, because rice can tolerate saturation.

Rice is a great "thriller" element for containers and can be grown as an alternative to the overused annual "purple fountain grass" *(Pennisetum setaceum* 'Rubrum'*)*. For years, I have been bored seeing it as the usual center plant in mixed containers, and am especially disappointed in its overall habit of collapsing in summer rainstorms. Though I love the deep-burgundy foliage of fountain grass, it seems to me that rice, specifically the ornamental cultivar 'Black Madras', makes an ideal replacement. This handsome black-leafed variety offers an upright habit with structural integrity.

RICE IN THE LANDSCAPE: With heavy summer rains here in North Carolina, we get a lot of downspout runoff – a problem that needed to be addressed. Since I love finding a plant-based solution to a common landscape challenge, I set out to find water-absorbing plants for each of my downspout areas around the house. Initially, I planted papyrus, the water-

After experimenting with rice seedlings, I've found that direct cultivation is what works best for me.

loving grass that the ancient Egyptians used to make paper. That was a great annual option, but over the years it had become difficult to source and was not winter hardy. Rice could be an ideal alternative. First, rice seed is easy and inexpensive to find through online retailers; second and third, the roots of the rice plants would absorb excess water while the seed offers a potential harvest. Win-win-win.

Along those lines, planting clumps of rice in the foundation landscape bed was an opportunity to test its cultural requirements. This full-sun bed had well-drained soil and required manual irrigation to ensure summer plantings would thrive. Additionally, I could learn more about the compatibility of rice with other garden favorites such as coleus, peanuts, peppers, sweet potatoes and zinnias.

I got straight to it, sowing seeds both in communal trays for transplant and directly in the ground and containers, to run a growing comparison. Within days, both methods had a high germination rate. The direct seeded clumps grew with great vigor and benefited from not having root disruption. After about three weeks, I transplanted the rest and watched with glee as they flourished through an exceptionally hot and wet summer.

HOW DID THAT FIRST YEAR GO? Through all of the experiments there were a few lessons learned. Direct seeding is my preferred approach to rice cultivation. Seeding in a tray and transplanting is an unnecessary step, and the transplanted clumps require a lot more supplemental irrigation. They also flowered and died much earlier compared to the clumps that were direct seeded, both in the ground and in containers. Another interesting observation related to growing rice in containers: The undrained pots work the best, because you can keep the plants fully saturated. Otherwise, plan to transplant your container-grown rice into large pots or into a wet area of your garden mid-season.

Every year since, I expand my summer rice production, making sure to site it near an easy–access water source. Rice is a thirsty plant, especially compared to other summer cereal crops like corn and sorghum.

COMPANION PAIRINGS: I find it is well paired with shrubs like paperbush *(Edgeworthia chrysantha)* and hydrangea *(Hydrangea macrophylla)*, both Asian natives that also prefer moist soil and mild climates.

Rice grains – almost ready for harvest

Summer annuals like *Callibrochoa, Duranta* and *Plectranthus* are also great companions because they thrive in the same cultural conditions in the ground or in a pot with drainage. With its fine texture, upright habit and dynamic foliage coloration, rice is an ideal option for every summer garden!

History

Rice has fed more people over a longer period of time than any other crop on Earth. Dating back to at least 2,500 B.C., rice as we know it today has been a staple in Asian cultures.

But the genus *Oryza* is among the most ancient grasses and was present when all the continents were one giant landmass known as Pangea. During this time, before the continents drifted apart, forming the world that we recognize today, ancient relatives of rice were able to spread throughout Pangea, resulting in many species that developed on multiple continents, including what would become Australia and South America. However, only two species were domesticated, *O. sativa,* the common species from Asia, and *O. glaberrima,* of Africa.

Rice is an integral part of folklore in many cultures around the world. Ancient tales, such as the Chinese legend of rice being a gift from animals, remain culturally relevant even today. The story begins after a devastating flood that destroyed all the plants, and famine was facing the population. One day, a dog ran through the flooded field and rice seed gathered in its fur. That seed was planted and the rice crops thrived, thwarting the threat of hunger and enabling generations to follow.

Folklore aside, there is no question of the historical significance of rice in the global agricultural market. When rice was introduced to the New World during Colonial times, it was quickly revered as an essential crop for the Southeast United States.

Did you know... the production of rice, not cotton or tobacco, was responsible for the initial wealth of Southern plantations?

Present Day

Today, 90% of the world's rice is cultivated in Asia and feeds more than 2.7 billion people annually. Because Asian rice production is so advanced, the lesser-known African species is difficult to source and has all but disappeared from modern cultivation, even in Africa. Despite that, rice is grown in more than 100 countries around the globe and serves as an essential source of income for millions of households.

Outside of food production, rice plants generate a lot of biomass in the form of straw and husks. With little commercial value, discarding these residues has caused considerable environmental damage, including air pollution from burning and methane emission from the incorporation of the biomass into soil. Innovative uses of these by-products offer new income opportunities and help to mitigate the effects of climate change. For example, rice hulls are now commonly used by American nurserymen as a means of suppressing weeds. Applied as a topcoat in container production, a one-inch layer of rice hulls can eliminate the need for the application of pre-emergent herbicides.

Cultural Requirements and Variety Selection

As a home gardener, you can plant rice throughout your sunny borders – no flooding needed. But one key to success is having easy access to water, since rice will suffer in dry soil.

As with all plants, especially grains, fertility is an essential aspect of plant health. In small

'Carolina Gold' rice planted at Chanticleer Gardens as a summer crop.

batches, this is easy to overcome. I add a handful of Plant-tone to every area that I sow, then once a month I water the growing rice plants with fish emulsion. It will thrive in the same soil and irrigation conditions as many summer favorites – several already named above, as well as begonias, sweet potato vine and others. Plant it where you can water it regularly or have an irrigation system in place. This will result in a lush crop with heavy seed set that looks beautiful all summer long.

Did you know... rice requires evenly moist soil – but not constant saturation? Rice is not a bog plant!

PESTS AND DISEASES? I have not experienced any pest or disease problems with my rice, which is not surprising when you are growing small quantities of a plant. However, Japanese beetles, the most common garden pest, can forage on the leaves. For commercial rice growers, there are more than 100 species of insects that are considered problematic; bacteria, fungi and viruses can also cause trouble. It is always a best practice to select a resistant variety to avoid the potential for crop loss.

Rice is susceptible to root knot nematodes, which I have throughout my garden. So far, I haven't detected their damage on my rice. This microscopic organism will invade the root system, causing root knot galls that drain the plant of its nutrients and result in lack of vigor and crop loss. So why haven't the nematodes discovered my in-ground rice plants? Probably because they are too busy infecting my heirloom tomatoes, okra and everything else! But this concern is why I cultivate rice in containers in addition to growing in landscape. My plan B.

GERMINATION AND GROWTH: Germination is fast, usually within seven days of sowing. That is because you are planting rice during the heat of the summer, and it requires warm soil for germination. You can pre-germinate seed in a greenhouse to get a jump on the season, but I prefer to direct sow my rice seed to avoid transplant shock.

The plants will develop leaves through the summer for 50-85 days after sowing, depending on the variety. At that stage, the reproductive panicle – aka flower stalk – will begin to emerge. This can be seen as a bulging of the leaf stem, known as the "booting" stage. This will continue to elongate, eventually revealing the bloom, which is referred to as "heading." Flowering technically begins one day after the heading has completed and can continue for about a week.

MATURITY: Like all grains, rice is wind-pollinated. As the flowers open, they shed their pollen abundantly, ensuring the entire panicle will produce viable seed. It generally takes about 30 days for the seed to fully mature, with weather playing a major role. In years with hurricanes and cloudy, wet conditions, it can take significantly longer for the rice seed to mature. As with any plant, the development of seed follows fertilization, and in rice there are several stages of ripening based on the texture and color of the growing grain. Terms like milky, dough, yellow, ripe and maturity all refer technically to the maturity stages. As a home grower, I have never needed to know any of that. I just watch the plant and feel the seed heads and it becomes quite obvious when the seed is ready to be harvested.

Selecting a variety from 40,000 different options could seem daunting, but as a home grower, you only have about ten selections to choose from. That's thanks to the expertise of online retail seed sources that comb through the cultivars and offer the seed that is best suited for small batch growing. I, for one, am relieved that I don't have to make any major decisions. When I see rice listed in a catalog, I know I'm safe to buy it.

VARIETIES: There have been a few standouts in my experience:

- 'Carolina Gold' is at the top of my list. This is a long-grain variety and was the basis for the Colonial antebellum economy of the coastal Carolinas and Georgia. It originated as an African and Asian hybrid strain and is unique because of its uncommon starch character and versatility of flavor. As a landscape plant, it is a strong grower with a height of about 36-42 inches tall. The foliage is yellow-green, and is particularly notable when grown side-by-side with other cultivars such as 'Blue Bonnet', which has dark green leaves.

'Black Madras' rice

- 'Black Madras' (mentioned above) is sold as an ornamental strain, though it sets edible seed. Compared to traditional agricultural rice selections, this black-purple leaf variety has a modest harvest and a much slower growing habit. But the foliage color makes up for it, which is why I recommend planting it first and foremost for its ornamental attributes.

Other varieties I have successfully cultivated include 'Duborskian' and 'Hayayuki', both sourced from Baker Creek Heirloom Seed. They performed very well in the conditions I provided: sun from 11am-4pm, and planted in fertile soil with daily watering. I am lucky to have saved my seed for planting the next season, because they are no longer listed in the current availability. My hope is that through this book more seed sources will begin to offer grains like rice so that these plants become a mainstream part of a home gardener's collection.

Final Thoughts

Overall, rice has become my top warm season grass to cultivate and I cannot imagine my garden, or my life, without it. I do not grow rice with the expectation of never again buying it from the grocery store. Rather, growing it has made me appreciate the accessibility that we have through commercial distribution. Like all of these grains, once you have cultivated, cared for, harvested and processed the crop, you will never take for granted these basic food sources. For me, that is the underlying gift of growing food.

Sorghum – The Sweetness
Sorghum bicolor

Sorghum

Introduction

Sorghum was an impulse buy, simply because I had no idea what it actually was. I first saw it while touring the inspiring grounds of Monticello, one of the best examples of heritage gardening in the U.S. The rows of tall stalks immediately caught my attention. They looked like corn, but just weren't quite right. I was intrigued and curious and wondered how I had never come across this beautiful, heat-tolerant summer annual.

I acquired seed from the gift shop, determined, because let's face it, if Thomas Jefferson grew it I needed to as well. That $2.50 investment was the start of an eye-opening journey exploring the beauty and functionality of a crop that has a long history in the world.

Growing sorghum was just a summer experiment as far as I was concerned. I didn't have any expectations for harvest; I just wanted to see it grow. Since I only had one packet with about 50 seeds in it, I was keen to space it appropriately to maximize the development. With my neighborhood garden helpers Abby and Aidan, we set out to convert the wave bed into a dynamic front yard display. Aidan carefully marked the bed every 14 inches with a divot three inches deep. Abby and I followed behind, dropping two seeds per hole. As a backup plan, in case the sorghum was a bust, we decided to add sunflowers to the border, dropping seed between the sorghum holes before gently raking over the bed and covering with two inches of triple shred hardwood mulch.

It was mid-June. This felt very late in terms of North Carolina growing, but as it turned out was perfect timing. Sorghum prefers hot soil and will germinate almost immediately when planted

My "living screen" of sorghum and sunflowers

in late spring, as the days are still increasing in light and temperature. Even so, I was shocked to see green leaves emerging from the ground just days after sowing and couldn't believe the rate of growth from week to week.

A LIVING SCREEN: Not six weeks after planting those seeds, the sorghum and sunflower border stood an impressive six-plus feet tall. From the front porch it provided an ideal screen from the street, which was yet another aha moment. When designing this property, I had hoped to create such screening, but I knew that using traditional shrubs would take years and ultimately create a lot of maintenance. Using summer annuals for this purpose was an inexpensive and interesting way to get instant gratification without the long-term work.

BIO-CONTROL TO THE RESCUE: As the canes swelled with sugar and the leaves stretched in the sunshine, amazing ecological transformations began to occur. It started with an infestation of aphids on the undersides of the sorghum foliage. Initially, I was determined to get rid of the aphids, until the voice of my dear friend Lloyd Traven, owner of Peace Tree Farm, an organic greenhouse in Pennsylvania, rang out: "Let nature take its course. Bio-control will happen if you let it." Sure enough, in the days that followed, the lady beetles descended to eat a robust meal of aphids. Native wasps, moths and viceroy butterflies came to feast on the "honeydew" that covered the tops of the leaves. In a matter of days, beneficial insects came from "nowhere" and cured my problem.

That was one of the most important lessons I have ever learned as a gardener, and it totally changed my approach to growing organically.

Meanwhile, our backup plan of sunflowers was flourishing. I recall falling to my knees upon seeing ALL the sunflowers open at once, lined like soldiers in the middle of my front yard. Neighbors stopped their cars in the street to take photos and friends gathered for selfies. This combination of sorghum and sunflowers was hands-down the most beautiful thing I had ever seen. It is remarkable how an investment of $2.50 and a few hours of bed preparation could captivate the attention of everyone who passed by.

With the ample rain and heat of a central North Carolina summer, the sorghum canes quickly rose to over ten feet tall with beautiful seed heads of varying colors. It was a sight I had never witnessed, and yet seemed appropriate for any sunny landscape. I couldn't help but ponder why the ornamental plant industry wasn't promoting this gem? And then, as those seeds ripened, another amazing thing happened: birds! Yes, birds of all kinds arrived in my front yard to feast on the ripe sunflower and sorghum seed, well above cat-catching range! That is when it hit me like a ton of bricks: I could grow my own birdseed!

THE BIRDSEED BONUS: It's funny, but in my 20 years as a professional horticulturist it had never once occurred to me. Thinking back to my childhood, we always bought birdseed. And later, I remember learning about all the pesticides that are applied to commercially available birdseed to ensure shelf life, and then I recalled the horrifying images of masses of birds falling from the sky after consuming seed that had been treated with a deadly systemic pesticide. Why on earth aren't we all just growing sorghum to feed our native "wildlife" (meaning birds, not raccoons, opossums, groundhogs and skunks!)?

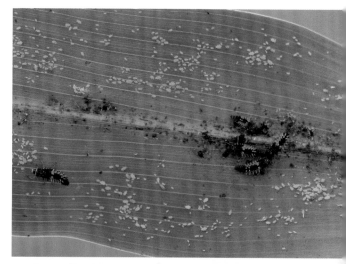

Biocontrol in action: (top) aphids and lady beetle larvae, and (bottom) viceroy and wasp.

DESIGN NOTES: Now I grow sorghum every summer in many different locations. I rely on it for seasonal screening in a back yard property border recently left bare after a hurricane knocked down an existing line of overgrown Leyland cypress. As I was discovering, sorghum makes a whole lot more sense for residential screening than a 60-foot conifer with a short lifespan. Sorghum is cheap and it doesn't require a backhoe to remove. It will grow to a size that is reasonable to cover things you don't want to see. It's fast but not permanent. It allows you to be creative each season and change your landscape to best meet your needs.

Another way to use sorghum as a design feature is to plant it as large clumps. Think pampas grass without the headaches! When your soil temperatures warm up in late spring, simply dig a hole about 15 inches wide by three inches deep and scatter the seed. Then cover it with compost and lightly mulch. The seed will germinate in place and grow until a hard frost nips it back.

THE BOTTOM LINE: Sorghum is a beautiful plant with great landscape interest, low input requirements AND it can feed those birds that most of us want to attract. So here I am, the Crazy Grain Lady on a mission to share what I've learned. What started as an aesthetic fascination has led me to a place of vast appreciation for all that these agricultural crops can offer to our living landscapes.

History

Dating back to 8,000 B.C., early domestication of sorghum was taking place in Northeastern Africa. There is archeological evidence that links it to the Egyptian-Sudanese border and from there it spread throughout the continent, adapting to the wide range of environments, including the highlands of Ethiopia and the semi-arid Sahel region south of the Sahara.

As with all the grains, people were the main catalyst for the movement of this cereal crop. Tribes and explorers are responsible for the global introduction of sorghum, which spread to India and China before making its way to Australia. It is likely that African slaves brought to the New World are responsible for transporting the seed and cultivating the earliest crops in America. Ben Franklin was the first person to mention sorghum-growing in the colonies, noting in 1757 its application for producing brooms.

Did you know... traditional brooms are made from "broom corn," a type of sorghum that will grow eight to ten feet tall? It has a long, strong brush or tassel.

Present Day

This African native grain ranks fifth in global cereal crop production and is of particular importance in regions afflicted with arid, drought-stricken conditions. In the past 50 years, cultivation of sorghum has increased by more than 60% and will likely become an even more important plant for both human and animal consumption in the future.

Sorghum is perhaps the most versatile cereal grain produced today, with the United States leading global production of grain sorghum. It is also among the most efficient plants for the conversion of solar energy and low water needs. Known as a high-energy, drought-tolerant crop, sorghum is considered the most environmentally friendly cereal grain produced.

Worldwide, sorghum has a lot of important uses including as a source of ethanol for bio-fuel. It is an essential crop in Africa, India and China with more than 75% of global production used for human consumption. Because it has a protein level of around 9%, sorghum can provide much-needed nutrition in times of famine and drought. In North America, sorghum is primarily grown as feed grain for livestock. Even the sweet varieties like I grow can be harvested for hay, pasture grazing and silage, in addition to their culinary uses.

A HEALTHY SWEET: Sweet sorghum is packed with many vitamins and minerals that we need to fuel ourselves. A one-tablespoon serving can supply about 15% of the Food and Nutrition Board's recommended daily allowance of manganese, which is required for energy metabolism and calcium absorption, among other things. It is also an important source of vitamin B-6, magnesium and potassium. Sweet sorghum is a healthy sugar!

Sorghum roots

Soil Benefits

Soil improvement is one of the greatest gifts that growing grains offer. And sorghum is one of the champs. It has a fibrous root system, similar to corn. However, these roots are more finely branched and considered more efficient at absorbing water and nutrients compared to corn.

They develop three types of roots structures, in sequence: First, the seminal or primary roots, which appear upon germination and anchor the plant into the earth. Then, after several weeks of growth, crown roots will form at the fourth leaf node. These aerial roots are thick and grow around the stalk and point directly down, ultimately penetrating the ground. Finally, brace roots grow, providing much needed structural integrity. It is because of this root adaptation that sorghum can grow upwards of 14 feet tall and not lodge, or break at the base, in windstorms.

The roots of sorghum do not penetrate as deeply as corn, but will reach three to four feet deep, providing excellent natural tilling properties to loosen hard-packed ground. Truly, the roots will do all the work for you, so put away your tillers and start gardening smart!

After frost you can either cut the stalks for harvesting or mow them back in place as a means of improving your soil. When left to decompose in place, the roots will provide additional organic matter to your native soil. This is a practice quite common in agriculture, but missing from today's landscape management techniques.

Cultural Requirements and Variety Selection

Because sorghum is a warm season, drought-tolerant crop that thrives in areas with hot temperatures and high humidity – more drought tolerant than other cereal grains – it gains added importance as we look to the future. Sorghum will appreciate a soil rich in organic matter, but will also grow in poor conditions. Full sun will result in the best growing habit, and though I have successfully grown it in part shade, the plants were significantly smaller and less productive.

It's best to wait to direct seed until several weeks after your last frost date, to ensure the soil has warmed to an appropriate temperature. This will give you fast germination and strong growth through the heat of the summer. In cooler climates with a shorter summer growing season, you can start plants indoors and transplant them into the garden.

N-P-K AT SEEDING: Since sorghum grows fast and creates a lot of biomass, fertility is an important consideration. Despite being tolerant of poor soils, if you want to get the most impressive development I recommend applying an even rate of N-P-K (nitrogen, phosphorus, potassium) when you sow the seed. That application will last through the entire growing season.

There are four main distinctions of sorghum varieties: grain, forage, biomass and sweet. I have only grown grain and sweet sorghum, both with great success.

GRAIN SORGHUM varieties come in all shapes, sizes and colors including red, orange, brown, tan and black. I recommend growing a shorter statured variety, which you often see growing in farmers' fields. Reaching only two to six

The flowers of sorghum are wind pollinated, which results in heavy seed set.

Dwarf grain sorghum seedheads ripening to a beautiful auburn color in the Serpentine at Chanticleer

feet tall, grain types are generally hybrids of Milo and Kafir. All sorghum varieties offer high ornamental appeal, but grain sorghum can produce large quantities of seed that can be used to feed birds, chickens, and you – it is delicious!

SWEET SORGHUM offers several benefits, including the production of sweet syrup. Unlike grain sorghum, the stalks of sweet varieties are grown for the purpose of being crushed, like sugarcane, to produce syrup. I grow it because it is tall and beautiful and the seeds feed the birds. One day I hope to crush enough to have a meaningful harvest, but it is well worth growing just for its low maintenance needs and ornamental appeal.

Final Thoughts

Sorghum changed my life as a gardener and I believe it will do the same for you. The many payoffs? The tall stalks with bright green flags of foliage will rise above any other annual in your garden. You can plant it in an area as a summer screen or use it, clumped, as a bold exclamation point. Either way, it will attract beneficial insects and provide nourishment for local birds. The sturdy roots prove hardy even against hurricane-strength winds, and ultimately provide aeration and structural improvement to the soil.

There is no logical reason that sorghum isn't already on your list for summer interest, so don't waste another season! Order your seed and discover the joy, ease and beauty of sorghum. ■

PART THREE

in the garden

Seven

Designing with Grains

*H*ere's how I think about designing with grains: I consider grains to simply be annual ornamental grasses. Nothing exotic or extraneedy about them. You can plant them in the same way you would grow commonly available grass specimens such as *Panicum, Miscanthus* or *Pennisetum*. The main difference is, at the end of the season you can eat the seed of the grain, whereas the ornamental grasses do not offer that added bonus.

Typical landscapes offer a lot of opportunities to experiment with seasonal grains. To start, you can identify open areas within your landscape borders. Even small spaces. Maybe a shrub has finally given up the ghost, or

you've been thinking of changing up some old plantings that haven't been looking so lovely in recent times. Voila...new spaces for your grain experiment.

Have you been wishing you didn't have so much lawn to tend? You might consider carving out some unneeded turf space and develop a larger bed that will allow you to cultivate a really meaningful harvest, like the wave bed that I described in Chapter 1.

FOCAL POINT OR MEADOW? There are two general approaches to integrating grains into a landscape. First is the traditional approach of adding clumps as architectural focal points.

This is typically how ornamental grasses are planted. For people living in neighborhoods with restrictive landscape covenants, this would be my recommended method. Everyone is accustomed to seeing clumps of ornamental grasses and therefore will likely not recognize the difference between traditional plants and grains.

The other way is *en masse*, as a meadow-like installation that covers a larger amount of space. This can be sown densely as a monoculture, mimicking a farmer's field, or mixed with seasonal companions to add color and interest, as seen in the photo above. This style is less formal and may not be appropriate for every front yard but is a very useful application when designing a large area for high impact.

Design Inspiration: Chanticleer Garden

One of the best examples of high impact grain design can be found at America's premier pleasure garden, Chanticleer, located outside of Philadelphia in Wayne, Pennsylvania. The grain bed, referred to as the Serpentine, is planted seasonally with different agricultural crops and is surrounded by perfectly manicured turf. Named for its sinuous lines, the Serpentine was inspired by a curvaceous farm road at Tuscany's 15th century Villa La Foce, whose rough, arid, hilly setting was reimagined in the 20th century into a lush, romantic environment by the British landscape designer Cecil Pinsent.

Chris Woods, the first Executive Director of Chanticleer and author of *Gardenlust*, encountered Villa la Foce on a trip to Tuscany and knew what he wanted to do back home: recreate at Chanticleer the villa's scenic hillside, with its upright Italian cypress accents and silver-foliaged olive trees surrounded by a groundcover of golden wheat. With a keen awareness of the farming history of the area, Chris set out to (as he said) "sculpt or paint with the crops that had once filled the region, but were now lost to development."

Over the years, the Serpentine has celebrated the aesthetics of agriculture with plants such as sorghum, wheat, rye, barley, sunflowers, tobacco, cotton, soybeans, rapeseed, crimson clover, kale, flax, rice and sesame. Just like a farmer's field, the crops are rotated, with a grain following a legume. Winter cover crops

Positioned along a slope, this nod to the land's agricultural past can be viewed from a distance for full impact. It was this vista that first captured my attention and served as a model for my front yard "grain wave."

are planted to help reduce erosion and build organic matter in the soil.

The grains are a magnet for birds indulging in the seeds. The year that sunflowers were planted, finches feasted for weeks, as did hawks on the finches. Though the Chanticleer Serpentine covers more square footage than most home gardens could devote, it is a planting to take inspiration from. What do I mean? Just consider how effective a nine-foot by three-foot curving bed of grains, flowers and vegetables might be and how you could influence local food production by taking back some of your existing turf area.

Chanticleer, and the talented gardeners who tend this property, are an endless source of motivation for me. Upon each visit I find myself

The true lesson of this planting is simple: A mass of one type of plant provides strong visual appeal. The curving shape increases the impact and the contrast with the common turf grass makes this an unforgettable installation.

To achieve this Tuscan look in eastern Pennsylvania's Zone 6, 'Emerald Sentinel' junipers and silver-leaved willows (Salix alba 'Britzensis') were sited. Espaliered gingkoes mimic the shape of a villa with a backdrop of big leaf magnolia and sugar maples that provide the ballast against the temporal planting.

gasping in awe of the beauty that is created through fine horticulture. It is always my goal to return home and implement at least a few of their innovative gardening ideas into my own landscape and I encourage you to plan a visit, and return frequently, as you will never be disappointed. Thank you to Bill Thomas, Executive Director and head gardener, David Mattern, Carla Hetzel, Eric Hsu, Jeff Lynch (Grounds Manager), Dan Benarcik, Przemyslaw Walczak, Lisa Roper, Chris Fehlhaber, Joe Henderson, Terry Struve, Scott Steinfeldt and Nate Pinelli for their vision, effort and inspiration.

Grains Design Inspiration #1

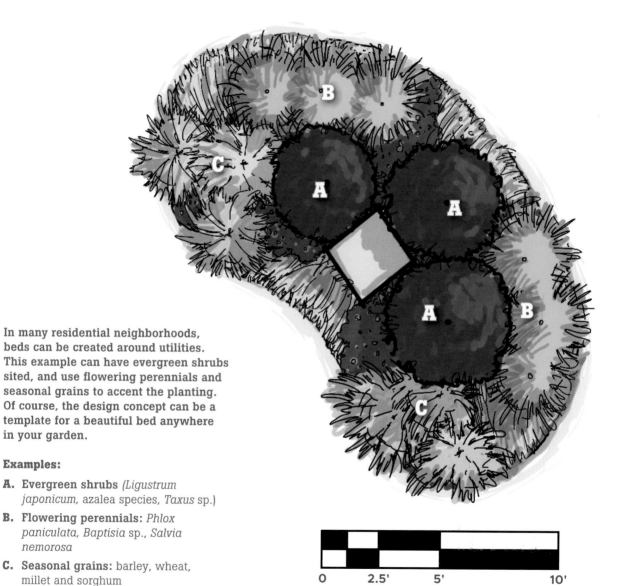

In many residential neighborhoods, beds can be created around utilities. This example can have evergreen shrubs sited, and use flowering perennials and seasonal grains to accent the planting. Of course, the design concept can be a template for a beautiful bed anywhere in your garden.

Examples:

A. **Evergreen shrubs** *(Ligustrum japonicum,* azalea species, *Taxus* sp.)

B. **Flowering perennials:** *Phlox paniculata, Baptisia* sp., *Salvia nemorosa*

C. **Seasonal grains:** barley, wheat, millet and sorghum

0   2.5'   5'   10'

Grains Design Inspiration #2

A foundation landscape offers an opportunity to add seasonal grains to contrast with the evergreen bushes and perennial flowers. Rice is an excellent choice to grow near a downspout through the summer.

Examples:

A. Large dark green – evergreen shrubs

B. Lavender and pink circles – flowering perennials like asclepias, phlox, salvia

C. Yellow circles – seasonal grains like rice or barley

D. Green circles – perennial grasses like carex or seasonal grains like millet or wheat

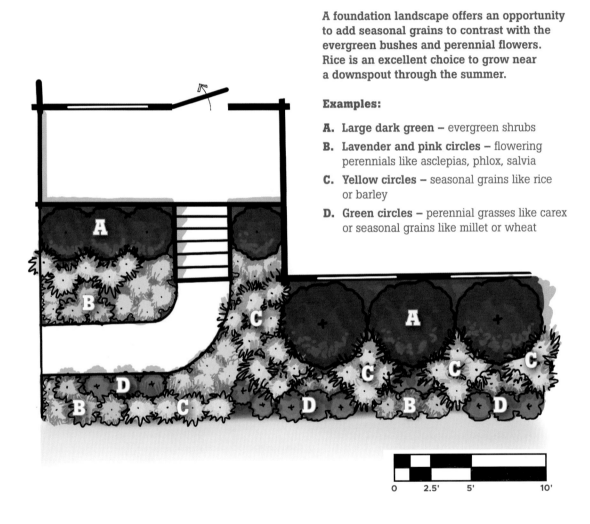

0   2.5'   5'   10'

Best Practices And Planting Tips

LET THE SUNSHINE IN: The key to successful grain cultivation is sun. I always say, there is a reason that farmers don't grow in the forest and that is because most edible crops need at least six hours of direct sunlight to flourish. Be sure to select areas that get full to part sun to ensure the best development over the course of a season.

Did you know... when grains are grown in too much shade, the plants will grow about half the size and the yields will be significantly less?

SOIL QUALITY: Grains are very useful as cover crops to help improve undernourished soil, but for the showiest display you will want to grow in fertile ground. This can be achieved by adding layers of organic matter, including ground-up leaves and well-drained compost. As these elements break down, the native soil will have increased porosity (drainage) and improved soil structure. The additional organic matter in the form of roots and decomposing stems and leaves will also increase microbial activity, which will naturally feed the plants and reduce your need for additional fertilizers.

WATERING: Soil considerations will play a role in your irrigation needs. Generally, the cool season grains require less water because they are growing during a period of time with lower temperatures and shorter days. However, the

warm season grains may need supplemental water as summer temperatures reach above 90°F, especially if you aren't getting abundant rain. The good news is, grains have some very obvious signs when they are drought stressed, namely the curling of their leaves and browning at the edges of the foliage. If your plants start to curl, give them an adequate drink of water to ensure they will keep looking beautiful for the entire growing season.

FERTILIZING: The addition of organic fertilizer is highly recommended. Grains have a robust growing habit and will utilize macro- and micronutrients in abundance. My first priority always lies in developing healthy soil. This will help reduce the need for adding fertilizer. However, upon planting/sowing I scatter a broad-spectrum organic fertilizer such as Plant-tone® to ensure my grains will have access to all the nutrients they require.

Other fertilizers that I recommend include powder formulations of poultry meal (also called feather meal) and water-soluble products such as fish emulsion. Both of these are rich in nitrogen. Cottonseed meal is another local fertilizer that I have had great success using, though it may not be available in areas outside the southeast United States.

My landscape beds are built from years of organic matter, which means I do not have to fertilize as often as you would in a newly developed landscape. Remember, grain crops are deeply rooted and they appreciate rich soil.

Did you know... if you top dress your beds with quality compost, you can reduce your long-term need for fertilizer applications?

Since all of the grains discussed in this book are annuals, you will have an opportunity to reinvent your landscape every six months (if you live in a mild climate such as USDA Zones 6-9). This allows you to be creative and experiment with different combinations and varieties. Year after year I never get bored, because my landscape always looks different.

Planting: Two Ways, Your Choice

Planting grains can be done by transplanting pre-germinated seedlings or by directly sowing the seed in the ground. Here's how to choose for your purposes.

WAY #1: If you are a beginner, or would just prefer not directly sowing the seed in the ground, you can grow your seeds in flats or pots. Then, when the roots become well established (meaning you can pull the seedling out of the pot without the soil falling apart), you can transplant the seedlings into your garden. This method works well but does require supplemental irrigation until the plants become established. The advantage is that you have full control over where the grains are planted and can easily create a very uniform, organized design.

WAY #2: Directly sowing the seed is very easy, albeit less common in today's gardening practices. It is an efficient method of growing that eliminates the step of transplanting. You can achieve the clumping look and avoid potential transplant shock or sow a large area to achieve the meadow design.

- To cultivate grains in clumps, dig a hole 3-4 inches deep by 12-24 inches wide and scatter the grain seed densely. Then cover it up and walk away. The grains will germinate within two weeks of sowing.

- If you prefer to create a meadow-like display, you will first need to loosen the soil before sowing. I like to use a hard rake, which will dig into the earth with its tines. This will ensure good seed-to-soil contact. To smooth the area after sowing I just turn the rake over and use the flat end. Unlike a soft-tined rake, which is ideal for moving leaves and lightly scratching the surface, hard rakes can be used as a sort of hand cultivator, while the long handle allows me to cover more ground without bending over.

When timed correctly, most grains will germinate within a few days of sowing. Because of this, it is best to mulch immediately after you plant the seed. I prefer triple shred hardwood mulch, as that will break down over time and add additional organic matter to your soil. Plus, I think it is important to make all your landscape beds match – and the addition of a light layer of mulch is visually appealing.

New to Seeding/Sowing? Fear Not...

Sowing seeds is always a big question I get when I talk to gardeners, because most people lack experience. The good thing about seed is it is inexpensive, so even if you are unsuccessful, it isn't a complete tragedy. However, I want to share some expert tips so you will have confidence when scattering your seed. (This information applies to all seeds, not just grain.)

BIG, IMPORTANT RULE: *First, evaluate the size of the seed.* This will help determine the best practices, including *stratification, scarification* and *planting depth.* Here's what all that means:

- Scarification is the process of breaking down the seed coat to speed up the germination process. The easiest way for home gardeners to scarify seed is by soaking them in hot tap water for 12-24 hours. The water only needs to be warm at the start. Store at room temperature while the seed is soaking.

Seed size determines sowing depth. Smaller seeds, like poppies, get surface-sown. Larger seeds, such as barley, sunflowers and corn, need to be incorporated in the soil.

- **Stratification** refers to a plant's need to have a temperature trigger to stimulate germination. This often is relative to soil temperatures. Cool season flowers and vegetables will germinate more readily when the soil temperatures are cool and damp. Some varieties actually need freezing and thawing to stimulate germination, which is why they need to be sown in late fall and allowed to grow in place with the cycles of the weather. In contrast, warm season plants require soil temperatures above 55°F for germination and establishment.

- **Planting depth** is best determined by the size of the seed. If you have a large seed, such as a sunflower, it will need to be planted deeper. Tiny seeds such as poppies require sunlight to germinate and therefore should not be covered at all. Everything in the middle can be lightly covered with soil and mulch. A good general rule of thumb is to determine planting depth by the seed size. The bigger the seed the deeper it should be planted. Most of the time one inch (or the depth of you pushing the seed into the soil with your thumb) is adequate.

Now, turn the page for a treat. In the next chapter I'll be showing off some excellent companion plants that will thrive alongside your beautiful grains. So much more beauty to tell you about! ■

Eight

Companion Plants that Play Well
(designing with flowering annuals, perennials, shrubs)

As home gardeners, we have the unique opportunity to grow edibles in a way that embraces diversity in the name of design and ecological functionality. Unlike large-scale farmers, we do not need to cultivate massive monocultures. We can take advantage of flowering annuals, perennials, shrubs and trees to create a beautiful landscape that provides relevant services for all aspects of life.

The idea behind foodscaping (the incorporation of edibles into a landscape) is simple: Just find an area that isn't planted and grow your favorite food crops. This idea extends to grains quite easily because they have such low maintenance needs. But no matter what is in your existing landscape, there is always an opportunity to fill in the gaps with a seasonal grain.

PLANTING FOR BIOLOGICAL DIVERSITY: One of the most important aspects of gardening is recognizing how to plant with a diverse selection of plants. Considering that all of the grains featured here are in the same plant family, *Poaceae*, it is critical that you add other plants to the mix. Not only will most of these companion plants produce beautiful flowers for you to enjoy, they will offer habitat and nectar to beneficial pollinators, who ultimately make your garden a living ecosystem.

WON'T YOU BE MY NEIGHBOR? Selecting appropriate companion plants for your grains is a very exciting process. I recommend that you start out with a simple palette so you don't feel overwhelmed. Over time, you will gain confidence and understand which plants do best in your environment. I rely on flowering annuals to accent my grain designs because the same seed-sowing cycle will apply. Also, these plants all share the same cultural requirements, making them ideal partners: They prefer full sun and garden soil with rich organic matter. It is also important to know that most prefer to be direct-seeded, as they do not thrive as transplants. One exception is for planting various edible greens; they can be either direct-seeded or first grown in pots and then transplanted to the garden.

Note: The companion list (right) gives a preview of the recommended plants I'll be featuring in the pages that follow. You'll notice that I have included several cereal and pseudo-cereal grain varieties along with the flowering options.

TO GROW WITH COOL SEASON GRAINS:

- Assorted Greens such as Arugula, Chard, Cilantro, Lettuce, Kale, and Mustard
- Bachelor's Buttons
- Clover
- Larkspur
- Love-in-a-Mist
- Poppies
- Root Vegetables such as Beets, Carrots, Parsnips, Potatoes, Radish, and Turnips
- Rye

TO GROW WITH WARM SEASON GRAINS:

- Amaranth
- Buckwheat
- Celosia
- Millet
- Peanuts
- Quinoa
- Sesame
- Sunflowers
- Zinnia

Companion Plants for Cool Season Grains

Cool season grain companions offer color and texture while attracting beneficial pollinators during the untraditional growing seasons with short days. The term cool season means just that: These plants prefer air and soil temperatures that are moderate; they can suffer in the heat of the summer. In northern climates these are great options for extending your season in early spring and late fall. In mild areas, like where I live, these plants will thrive through the winter months, being sown in November and blooming through April and May.

Cilantro flowers are attractive and edible.

Many of these combinations include flowering specimens and delicious edibles that can be harvested throughout the growing season. These recommendations all fall into the "old-timey" category, being plants that have proven their value over many generations. I have been growing all of these varieties for more than 20 years and I assure you they are reliable, inexpensive and provide a unique show that will impress everyone!

Assorted Greens
Amaranthaceae, Apiaceae, Asteraceae, Brassicaceae families

This is a broad category including leafy cool season greens like arugula, chard, cilantro, lettuce, kale and mustard. The goal here is to utilize the edible greens through the growing season and then allow them to bolt and flower. The flowers attract a diversity of beneficial insects and provide a dynamic color addition to the traditional spring flowers and grain seed heads.

Greens can be directly seeded into the landscape or transplanted from pots. My preferred method is to mix a bunch of different greens seeds into a bag and then "sprinkle the pixie dust" of the seed mixture onto the freshly raked soil. They will germinate quickly; if they seem too crowded, you can harvest to thin.

Crimson clover and buckwheat

Bachelor's Button
Centurea centureana, Asteraceae family
The bush-like habit of bachelor's button makes this a great accent specimen. The small, button-like flowers can range in color from the traditional blue, to maroon, lavender and pink. With silver-green foliage, the plants can easily grow to three inches tall and two feet wide when planted in rich garden soil. The blooms are ideal as a cut for flower arrangements. Bachelor's buttons transplant easily, and once established can self-sow. In fact, I rarely have to reseed now, as this annual reappears every fall and grows into robust clumps that bloom for more than six weeks!

Did you know... at one time it was a custom for bachelors who were pursuing a sweetheart to wear a bachelor's button?

Crimson Clover
Trifolium incarnatum, Fabaceae family
A member of the legume family, crimson clover is a showstopper! The bright-red blooms attract beneficial pollinators while the roots help fix nitrogen for future crops. Crimson clover is a traditional cover crop, commonly planted after a cereal grain is harvested to add nitrogen to depleted soil.

A wonderful addition to the front of a sunny border, clover is easy to grow from direct seeding. In mild climates it is best grown as a cool season plant, seeded in late fall for a spring bloom. I cut my clover down before the seeds ripen so I have better control over where it will grow.

Larkspur
Delphinium elatum, Ranunculaceae family
Larkspur is one of those annuals that you may first notice thanks to a mass planting adjacent to a highway. The brilliant blue-violet flowers can be spotted at 75 mph! I have long admired the seed-cultivated roadside displays and have used those plantings as inspiration for my home gardening methods.

Note of caution: Larkspur is especially practical (with caution), as the foliage is poisonous and will help deter browsing mammals such as deer, groundhogs and rabbits. However, due to its toxicity I recommend planting this in areas where you will not mistakenly harvest the leaves. Though I have never had any trouble with pets eating it, I recommend you keep it out of reach of small children.

Everyone who visits my garden in May falls deeply in love with larkspur, and they all want it right then. It is important to know that larkspur does not transplant, so you have to directly sow the seed. It also needs cold to germinate – it is a cool season flowering annual. Here in central North Carolina, I sow mine at Thanksgiving. It germinates within a month of sowing. As temperatures warm, the stalks will grow to about four feet tall. Larkspur is a heavy seeder. In my garden it can self-sow densely, so some thinning may be required once you have an established patch.

Love-in-a-Mist

Nigella sativa, Ranunculaceae **family**
Another heritage flower, love-in-a-mist looks much like the name implies. The soft, fern-like foliage accents the white or blue flowers. The stature of this flowering annual is significantly smaller compared to many others and is best suited near the front of a border. The jet-black seeds are encased in a balloon-like structure that turns tan and will open small slits when the seeds fully ripen.

Did you know... love-in-a-mist is also known as black caraway, and its seed can be ground into a seasoning?

Like poppies and larkspur, nigella is best directly sown during the cool season and allowed to germinate in a bright, sunny place. Because it develops a deep taproot, they do not transplant well. Once you have a patch established, expect some self-sowing. This is a delightful flowering annual that behaves well and can easily be incorporated into perennial borders to help fill in gaps during the spring.

Poppies
Papaver somniferum, Papaveraceae **family**

I love all poppies, but I have a special devotion to the old-fashioned "birdseed" varieties that I was introduced to as an intern at Montrose Gardens. They provide one of the most dynamic displays of mid-spring and I simply cannot imagine my garden without them. The soft-green lettuce-like foliage stands out while the flower stalks can reach up to four feet tall. Every stage of the poppy flower is noteworthy, from emergence to drying. Poppies offer architectural value and color while being an easy and inexpensive plant to fill in open areas of mulch space.

There are many different variants of poppies. The typical form has a single row of petals with a rainbow of colors to choose from, ranging from bright-red, salmon, deep-purple, lavender, pink and white. There are many fancy double forms with pom-pom-like petals. These are available from various seed suppliers, including Baker Creek Heirloom Seeds. If you are seeking a specific color or flower type, I recommend buying the seed each year from a reputable supplier. That way, you can be sure that you will get the exact color you want. Why? Because when you collect your own open-pollinated seed you will never know what the next generation will look like. In my case, I do collect and save the seed every year, because I love the surprise of seeing what comes up next in a range of colors and petal forms.

Fancied by a wide variety of pollinators, especially honeybees, the poppy flowers have a short duration of bloom, but the vibrant colors

are unmatched by any other plant. After the petals fall you can watch the seed head swell and ultimately dry. When the small "windows" open on the dried seed head, that is the sign that the seed is ripe and can, if you desire, be collected for the following year.

Just like larkspur, poppies do not transplant. Directly sowing the seed in the cool season is necessary. Poppy seeds also require light to germinate, meaning they have to be on the surface of the soil. My best advice for growing poppies is to sow them last, after the grains and other flowering annuals, so you don't step on them and push them into the soil. Do not cover them with soil or mulch, as that will impede their germination. Once established, they can self-sow, but that usually happens along bed edges, in gravel pathways and in the cracks of your driveway – never where you want them to grow! I re-sow my last season's seed at Thanksgiving, to ensure I have the display I desire for the following spring. In cooler climates you can wait until March or April. I have heard of people tossing the seed into beds covered with snow, which resulted in late spring germination and a beautiful display in summer.

Root Vegetables: rotate them in!

Apiaceae, Brassicaceae, Solanaceae families

The rotation of root vegetables in the landscape provides many benefits, including an ongoing replenishing of the soil's health. Their deep taproots penetrate compacted soil, help increase drainage and improve soil structure. Rotation is frequently used in farming practices.

Varieties such as carrots, parsnips, potatoes, radish and turnips are easy to grow from direct seeding. Direct seeding is necessary, since these root vegetables do not transplant well. The roots can be harvested over a long period of time through the growing season. Be sure to leave some plants in the garden and allow them to flower and set seed. The pollen will support many beneficial insects and the flowers create a beautiful display, especially when woven among cool season grains.

In cooler climates they will thrive all summer. Here in my Zone 7 garden, I grow plants in this category September-May.

Rye

Secale cereale, Poaceae family

I have included rye in the section of grain companions, not because I've been growing it and have had great success with it, but because 1) it's so good looking, and 2) of all the cool season cereals, rye is the only one I ever see growing in my region. It is very tall in stature and has stately silver-blue foliage. Though it is primarily grown as hay for animal feed in North America, rye is a staple in central and northern European cuisine.

In years past, I thought I was growing it, but it turns out "rye grass," which is commonly over-seeded in warm season turf, is not the same as the rye we eat! (But it *is* a *Poaceae* family member.) To be fair, I haven't searched very hard for proper rye seed. It wasn't readily available from any of my usual sources and I then forgot about it. Rye has never been a grain that I have enjoyed eating, despite my mom's best efforts to serve it with corned beef on St. Patrick 's Day.

Rye grows like the other cool season cereals, in full sun, and thrives in mild temperatures. Farmers in central North Carolina plant it in late fall and by April the flowers are visible from a passing car. In northern regions, rye can be sown in early spring for a mid-to-late summer harvest.

I plan to do my research and locate several varieties of rye for the upcoming season. Alas, that is the tale of every gardener – hope springs eternal and the cycle is endless.

Companion Plants for Warm Season Grains

These warm season companions thrive in the heat of the long days of summer. No matter where you live, these options are best planted after your last frost date and will grow through the heat of June-September. All of these varieties are frost sensitive, so do not be surprised to see them shriveled after your first cold snap of fall.

Several of these companion plants actually fall into the pseudo-cereal category and can be harvested and utilized as gluten-free culinary options. These tried-and-true varieties all prefer full sun and evenly moist soil – the exact-same conditions as their grain counterparts. I highly recommend direct seeding these, though you can transplant if you feel more comfortable.

Did you know... a pseudo-cereal is not a grass at all, and therefore not a member of the *Poaceae* family? But it can be used like a cereal grain, most commonly when ground for flour. Amaranth, buckwheat, chia and quinoa are all pseudo-cereals that grow through the warm season and offer beauty and bounty to visiting pollinators and gardeners alike.

Different varieties of amaranth provide brilliant color in these pots at Denver Botanic Garden.

Amaranth 'Dreadlocks' has unique ornamental appeal.

Amaranth
Amaranthus sp., Amaranthaceae family
I originally grew amaranth with the intention of harvesting the seed to eat. After watching the enormous flower heads develop, I became quite paranoid that all that ripening seed could become too invasive for my maintenance practices. So I cut the flowers off before the seed had a chance to ripen. Though I thought I had been careful, I still had several thousand seedlings the following year, which I painstakingly removed by hand as they germinated. I share that bit of advice not to scare you away from growing it, but so you'll be fully aware of what can happen. Nevertheless, amaranth, a pseudo-cereal, is a gorgeous plant with many colors and growing habits available. I still grow it, but keep it in areas that could easily be mowed if seed escapes captivity!

I have always directly sown amaranth because the seeds are so small and it seems tedious to grow large numbers of individual seedlings in pots for later transplant in the garden. However, if you only want a few specimens you will have better control with transplants.

Buckwheat
Fagopyrum esculentum, Polygonaceae family
Buckwheat is high on my list of favorite summer annual flowers. It should be planted in every single sunny garden. The bright white flowers of the straight species glow through the heat of the summer, attracting more than 20 different species of pollinators! Growing to about two feet tall, plants develop quickly, usually blooming within 30 days of direct seeding. They are well behaved and mingle with a wide variety of summer-active plants, including flowering perennials and shrubs. With excellent heat and drought tolerance, buckwheat is a practical, beautiful plant to include every summer.

Growing buckwheat is easy: You can directly seed it like I do, or grow it in pots and transplant it. Once you have it established it will self-sow. But it is not terribly aggressive and is easy to pull out. Personally, I am charmed by it and love to see it spread around in my garden.

This pink-flowered buckwheat can be purchased from online retailers.

Celosia or Cockscomb

Celosia cristata, Amaranthaceae **family**

Also known as cockscomb, celosia is an old-fashioned cut flower that is a reliable source of color all summer long. Over the years, I have gravitated toward the straight species form that is not crested and has a taller growing habit. With a wide range of colors in both flowers and foliage, this is a standout annual that every gardener should grow.

It is worth noting that celosia, like amaranth, will self-sow readily, often right along a bed edge. It will transplant, so feel free to dig out the rogue seedlings and relocate to a better spot in your landscape.

Millet

Pennisetum glaucum, Poaceae **family**

Millet is a true cereal grain and is included here in spite of my lack of experience growing it, and because it is a most worthy grain. I have made the mistake in the past of purchasing millet plants at garden centers, which seem to only live a few weeks once transplanted in the garden. Those "ornamental" millets have beautiful colored foliage, but with a short lifespan they might seem like a waste of time.

This summer I have finally invested in proper seed of dwarf pearl millet and plan to sow a large plot with the intention of feeding the birds. I feel confident that it will thrive with direct seeding; after all, that is exactly how the farmers grow it! Full sun is a must for this heat-loving grain. It is well adapted for drought, though supplemental irrigation is appreciated in extreme conditions.

Millet is a multi-tasking plant: It brings beauty to your garden, helps out the birds, and produces large, puffy-looking seed heads that look great in dried arrangements. This is another "stay tuned" crop for me and I am excited to add this to the garden for years to come.

'Purple Majesty' millet growing at Chanticleer.

Peanuts

Arachis hypogaea, Fabaceae **family**

Simply stated, peanuts are awesome! My favorite summer groundcover. They are the heat and drought tolerant legume of my dreams, and since I started thumbing raw peanuts into open areas, my garden has an added layer of shock, awe and purpose.

I realize peanuts may not work for everyone, as they really do love HOT soil temperatures and thrive in sandy soil. They are a staple agricultural crop in my region, which is why I started to grow them. In colder areas you can start the seed indoors in pots and then transplant them after your last frost date.

They are excellent in large containers because that soil will heat faster than in the ground, and you will likely get a small harvest before frost nips them back in fall. For those of you gardening in warm regions, plant peanuts anywhere you have open space in full sun. They have very low maintenance needs, and the little, pea-like yellow flowers are pretty.

In recent years, I have under-planted *Asclepias tuberosa* (butterfly weed) with peanuts and have found monarch chrysalises attached to the underside of the pinnate foliage. One of the most unique characteristics of the peanut relates to its botanical name: *Hypogagaea* means "underground" in Latin and refers to the pod development, which is atypical for a legume crop. Known as "geocarpy," the edible nuts actually form in the ground, from a structure called a peg, which initiates off the above-ground stems. If you have never seen this in person it truly is a sight to behold. From toddlers to adults, peanuts will captivate garden visitors of every experience level.

Quinoa
Chenopodium quinoa, Amaranthaceae family

Without question, quinoa (pronounced keen-wah) is the hottest "super food" to hit grocery stores shelves. Celebrated as a gluten-free, nutrient-dense pseudo-cereal, quinoa is showing up as an ingredient in all kinds of foods, even cookies.

Growing quinoa has been a serious challenge for me. I have yet to have a successful experience, despite trying every season. The best crop I have seen was planted at the Dallas Arboretum and was in full-seeded glory at the end of October. I still cannot understand how it could thrive in Dallas and not in Raleigh, but alas, the plant has escaped my capacity to grow. Nevertheless, I will keep trying, as it is a beautiful plant that offers so much for the home garden.

Perhaps starting the seed in a tray or pot in a controlled environment is a better approach. Then you can transplant into the garden once the roots are well established. I have only direct seeded in my home garden and have literally gotten no germination. This seems like a great opportunity for growers and garden centers to sell to curious consumers.

The bottom line is, sometimes plants just don't cooperate, which only makes me want to grow it more. All sources indicate quinoa prefers the same conditions as amaranth: full sun, well-drained soil with supplemental irrigation through the heat. I have no intention of losing interest and will continue my quest to cultivate quinoa one day!

Sesame
Sesamum indicum, Pedaliaceae family

Sesame is hands-down my favorite summer annual – probably the most underutilized plant of this era. I first saw this planted at Monticello and was immediately fascinated. I had never seen sesame before; in fact, I don't think I had ever thought about sesame as a plant. It was just that seed on hamburger buns. Turns out, this native to India is an ideal plant for hot, humid regions and can reach upwards of six feet tall in good soil. It blooms all summer and looks like a foxglove on steroids.

White-seeded sesame has a pure white flower and dark-seeded sesame has a pink bloom. You need to grow both! As fall approaches, the seeds will develop along the tall stalks and ultimately turn brown when fully ripe. You can simply cut the stalk off and shake the seed out into a bucket and store for next season, or process into oil or tahini, depending on how ambitious you are!

Sesame is very versatile and can be grown as a transplant or from direct seeding. Now that it is well established in my garden, I find seedlings germinating, and if growing in the wrong spot they can be moved with little effort.

Sunflowers
Helianthus **sp.**, *Asteraceae* **family**

Who doesn't love sunflowers? A garden is just not complete without the addition of the classic summer bloom. Since it is the world's easiest plant to grow, I recommend planting large quantities in succession to maximize the show. I start direct seeding after my last frost date and plant once a week for six to ten weeks. That will ensure that I will have blooms for over a month! Of course, sunflowers attract beautiful pollinators, and once the seed ripens you will find that a wide variety of birds will quickly

devour the seeds. That is another reason to grow a lot and plant over a period of several weeks. You can extend your bird-feeding season and ensure that you will be able to save some seed for your next season.

Sunflowers are another example of a plant that readily self-sows and can be transplanted with ease. If you have ever purchased birdseed, you have likely had a few sunflowers sprout near your feeder. You can dig them and move them into an area where they can grow into their full glory.

As their name indicates, sunflowers thrive in bright conditions. They can grow upwards of 12 feet tall in rich garden soil, but you can grow varieties that are shorter if preferred. My go-to variety is 'Mammoth' because I like their tall stature and am confident that even my agile kitten will not be able to reach a feeding bird.

Zinnia
Zinnia elegans, Asteraceae **family**

An essential flower of summer, zinnias offer an abundance of color for a long duration of time. I recommend selecting cultivars that have resistance to powdery mildew, as that will ensure the best-looking specimens and the longest bloom cycles. I grow zinnias not only for their accent in the landscape but also as cut flowers to make my house feel bright and cheerful. They are an outstanding cut specimen because they don't make a mess even as they fade. I have never gardened without zinnias, and I have been known to scatter seed of this resilient plant in public landscapes simply

because I believe no summer garden should be without this cheerful bloom.

Since zinnias have been a warm season staple in my garden for eight years, seedlings will appear throughout my borders. If you want a specific variety, purchase seed and either directly sow or grow them out in pots and plant them into the garden when they reach four inches tall.

Harvesting and Storing Seed for Grains and Your Annual Companion Plants

Harvesting and storing seed is well worth your time and effort. The information in this section applies to grains, but also to some of the less common companion plants (especially annuals) that you might not find in a nursery. Storing seed ensures that you will have ample supply for the following season at no cost. It is also a great way to get up close and personal with your seed, which will provide you valuable insights. I swear, the more time you spend with a plant the better you will be at growing it.

HARVESTING BASICS: Harvesting seed is a bit of a waiting game. You don't want to harvest seed that isn't fully ripe. Be sure to wait until the plant has completely died, aka dried out. That will make collection a breeze, as the seed will easily release from the pod. Gather the seed into a secure container such as a bucket or a bag. Many seeds are best harvested *en masse* and then may need to be lightly winnowed, which is just a fancy way of saying remove the large particles before storing.

Did you know... the easiest way to winnow small batches of seed is to just blow on them? The seeds tend to be heavy and will settle at the bottom, and the chaff will float away.

BEST ADVICE FOR SEED STORAGE: Keep it dry, dark and refrigerated, not frozen! This will guarantee the longest shelf life. Generally speaking, it is best to sow seed within six to eight months of harvesting, as that is its prime viability. Of course, I have been known to hoard seed for years – with proper storage it can germinate long after its estimated expiration date.

My favorite storage vessel is a Talenti Gelato container, because I like to reuse plastic and I love to eat the delicious frozen dessert! The screw-on lid is easier to use than a zipper bag and the clear plastic container is ideal for seeing the seed and writing on, to remember what you collected and when. They also fit perfectly on a refrigerator shelf and are large enough to store a meaningful amount to sow the next season – or share!

Companion Perennials and Shrubs

With thousands of beautiful perennial ornamental plants in the marketplace, it is impossible for me to get too specific. However, I want to provide you some general plant pairings that have worked very well for me. All of these suggestions are based on mixing ornamental plants with food crops that have the same cultural requirements: sun, fertilizer and water.

Flowering Perennials & Friends

These plants offer a lot of appeal, from their beautiful blooms to providing nectar for pollinators. They all prefer full sun and evenly moist soil and are hardy in Zones 5-9. (Shown with suggested favorite playmates.)

Anise hyssop – Agastache foeniculum: wheat, buckwheat, chard, lettuce, radish

Blue false indigo – Baptisia australis: barley, cucumber, mustard, squash, watermelon

Butterfly weed – Asclepias tuberosa: rice, corn, basil, okra, peppers

Catmint – Nepeta faassenii 'Cat's Meow': barley, amaranth, rye, potatoes, zucchini

Joe-pye weed – Eutrochium purpureum: barley, corn, sorghum, amaranth, buckwheat

Mountain mint – Pycnanthemum muticum: oats, sorghum, okra, peanuts, sesame

Ornamental onion – Allium 'Millenium': oats, beets, cilantro, eggplant, kale

Phlox – Phlox paniculata: rice, beans, carrots, kale, turnips

Purple coneflower – Echinacea purpurea: sorghum, millet, chard, herbs, tomatillo

Woodland sage – Salvia nemorosa 'Violet Riot': wheat, arugula, peanuts, sesame, sweet potatoes

Well-Tamed Shrubs

Shrubs offer important structure in the landscape in addition to flowering at different times of the year. I love shrubs because their maintenance needs are very low. When sited with enough space they will require very little pruning and have deep roots, making them more drought tolerant. Unlike herbaceous perennials (that die back every year), shrubs do not have to be cut back to the ground every year. Appropriate spacing is an important consideration, something I do not do well.

Hydrangea paniculata 'Sweet Summer' and Phlox paniculata 'Bright Eyes' bloom all summer and attract pollinators.

Often, the information on the plant tag is not accurate, so before you trust that "mature size" listed on the label, do research for how a variety performs in your area. Below is a list of well-behaved shrubs that will grow to under six feet tall with limited pruning.

Like the flowering perennials above, these shrubs prefer more sun than shade. Once established, they will require very little care. However, I always recommend fertilizing every plant in your landscape once a year with a light application of a well-balanced organic fertilizer to ensure best performance.

You will notice I have left off cultivar recommendations. That is simply because there are so many great ones to choose from. Your call!

Abelia – *Abelia grandiflora*

Beautyberry – *Callicarpa americana*

Forsythia – *Forsythia intermedia*

Japanese Snowball aka Viburnum – *Viburnum plicatum*

Panicle hydrangea – *Hydrangea paniculata*

Smooth hydrangea – *Hydrangea arborescens*

Summersweet – *Clethra alnifolia*

Virginia sweet spire – *Itea virginica*

Winterberry – *Ilex verticillata*

Witch alder – *Fothergilla gardenii*

"But is it Deer Proof?"

*I*t's a question on so many gardeners' minds. If you have ever been in a presentation of mine you know I have some creative ideas for dealing with browsing mammals. But to answer the question, *Is it deer proof?* NO! No plant is entirely "deer proof," a term that generally refers to any wildlife that snacks on your plants. I promise, the moment you start to feel confident that you have outsmarted them, they will prove you wrong. And somehow these animals seem to know how much you spent on a plant! The bigger the investment, the more likely they will eat it to the point of no return.

THE CREATURES YOU HAVE… As I have traveled the country I have come to realize I have it pretty easy where I live. Sure, we have deer, rabbits, groundhogs and squirrels, but that's nothing compared to wild hogs, bears or antelopes! A friend once declared to me – predicted – that I would French kiss a deer the day the armadillos make it to my garden! Did you know armadillos are making their way north and east? Yep, these meat eaters don't actually browse your plants but rather dig holes everywhere in search of grubs and other ground-living insects. So, appreciate the creatures you have, because it could always be worse!

To really dive into this topic, which all gardeners seem to share an interest in, we have to first think about why we have the wildlife pressure in our residential developments. During an inspiring and insightful lecture by master naturalist and author Nancy Lawson, my eyes

A once in a lifetime deer hug while touring gardens in Tarboro, NC.

were opened to the importance of being a better steward – not just to the land I cultivate but to the wildlife that my neighborhood displaced. It's a conundrum: On one hand it is annoying to have my garden eaten by a herd of passing deer. But think about it – we tore down their home (nature) to build ours. Then we eliminate the native plants they had lived on and replace them with exotic specimens that are irrigated and fertilized, growing plump and lush. Of course they are going to eat from our landscapes – it's a smorgasbord!

H **IS FOR HELP!** Have you ever heard that deer love every plant that starts with an H? It's true! *Hosta, Hydrangea, Heuchera, Hemerocallis* (daylily): all deer candy. There are plenty of ornamental plants that will keep browsing mammals happy, but when you add food crops like grains to your landscape, a whole new world of wildlife management can occur.

See, we aren't the only ones who like to eat grains! Turns out, all creatures love them. I have yet to meet an animal who didn't express some interest in my cereal crops, from my over-indulged house cats (who do nothing to manage the invading wildlife, but love to eat the fresh leaves of oats) to rabbits, groundhogs and yes, deer. Over the past 20 years of gardening I have tried just about everything. Many of the most effective strategies are cost prohibitive, like installing a ten-foot-high deer fence around your property, with chicken wire buried two feet deep to keep out armadillos, rabbits and groundhogs. Not only is that expensive, but for most people living in suburban developments, it isn't allowed!

MY NOT-TO-DO LIST: There are some things you simply should not do because 1) they don't work, and 2) you actually create a bigger problem. One example is the notion of stringing clear fishing line around your garden at ankle height. Unless your goal is to send your husband to the emergency room (no offense, guys, but you often don't look where you walk), you will find that the deer can and will step right over it to eat whatever precious plants you are trying to save.

And then there is putting fine black mesh over plants, especially close to the ground. More often than not, a curious snake will make its way into that netting. If you have never had to cut a snake from mesh, consider yourself fortunate. It is stressful for both parties and if you do not aid in the rescue the snake will die. This is totally unnecessary, as many snakes play vitals roles in managing the mammal population that we are at odds with.

My favorite critter strategies

I'd like to share some advice on practical, cost-effective strategies that I have employed with success to manage a wide variety of hungry visitors over the years. One of the key components is to first identify what animal is causing the damage. Most gardeners deal with a variety of visitors at different times of the year. For instance, deer tend to be most problematic in fall during rut, when males are rubbing the velvet from their antlers. This is when you see major damage to small-caliper trees and shrubs. Spring and summer tend to be when heaviest deer browse occurs,

as mothers teach their fawns to navigate through your neighborhood. The rabbits and groundhogs also seem to be big spring and summer eaters, whereas the squirrels are busy digging through fall and winter.

REPELLENTS: The type of repellent I would recommend depends on just who it is you're wanting to repel. A general "deer spray" doesn't necessarily work for deterring rabbits, squirrels or that neighborhood dog that uses your mailbox planting as a toilet every day. To successfully use repellent you need to apply a formulation that is specific for the animal you are trying to deter. That is why I love the I Must Garden line of animal repellents. Not only do these animal-specific concoctions work, they actually smell good so none of your neighbors will be offended.

WATER SURPRISE! Motion-sensor irrigation is a great way to deter browsers, especially at night. You do need an irrigation system, as you can buy the sprinkler and attach it to a hose that can be moved daily to add an additional element of surprise. The idea is simple: Just like a motion light, the irrigation sensor is triggered by movement. A sudden burst of water will shoot out, thus spooking the intruder – both animal and human. But be sure to turn it off if you are throwing an evening dinner party!

PLANTS THAT REPEL: Plants can also offer a practical solution. Consider specimens with large thorns and a low, branching habit, such as the hardy citrus *Poncirus trifoliata* 'Flying Dragon' (Zones 5-9) to help block deer runs and direct other animals around your property. For those of us in warm climates, agave can add an extra layer of protection, but be careful because those spikes hurt!

Flowering annuals with a strong scent, like lantana, in both the bush and groundcover form, will drive a nibbling rabbit to the next county! And traditional herbs are also great deterrents. It seems people are the only ones who enjoy the flavor of rosemary, thyme, sage and oregano. Many seasonal edibles are also effective at discouraging grazing mammals.

Did you know... garlic bulbs will help ward off moles and voles? And small-leaf varieties of basil will put off rabbits due to the bitter flavor of the leaves?

Again, I never say any plant is "deer proof," because as soon as I make that declaration a herd will prove me wrong. However, I will say there are a number of plants that can help reduce browsing damage from all the common culprits. By growing these plants along your bed edges, you just may be able to trick the critters into leaving your property and taking up residence in someone else's yard!

THE OLD BED-EDGE TRICK: Bed edges offer the ideal location to deter animals, because it is the first area they come to. If they sniff or taste something that isn't appealing, they tend to depart the premises. Bed edges are also convenient for watering and harvesting. I have found that many of the most practical food crops I grow for daily eating (which I plant as bed edges) are the best for warding off the troublemakers. Turn the page for my favorites that do double duty for me.

Walking onions will multiply, creating a dense layer along the edge that deters both in-ground and above-ground mammals.

Seasonal Edibles For Your Bed Edges

Just like with the grains, I distinguish my seasonal edibles into two categories: cool season and warm season. Cool season crops are best planted between September and March and harvested from November through May. Warm season crops thrive during the frost-free months, and are best planted in April and June with expected harvests from July through October. For gardeners in colder climates, you can plant all of these through the summer and enjoy the full benefits at once!

Plant a cool season edge
Arugula
(Eruca versicaria)

This cool season green will add spice and flavor to your salad and can be served "wilted" to complement hearty dishes. Grown easily from seed, arugula looks great planted *en masse* along a border edge, making harvest easy and convenient. Though people covet the flavor, rabbits and groundhogs are extremely offended by it, making this a top candidate for growing. I recommend directly sowing the seed along a sunny border in a light layer of compost. It will germinate quickly and the leaves can be harvested at every stage of development – even when it flowers! As the summer heat kicks in, allow the seeds to ripen, ensuring you will have another crop when temperatures moderate.

Allow your freshly harvested garlic bulbs to dry in the sun.

Garlic grows from a vegetative division that is best planted in fall throughout North America. I usually give a broad window for planting: Labor Day till Christmas! This will ensure the bulbs develop for an early summer harvest.

Planting garlic is fun. Just thumb in the raw individual cloves without removing the paper covering. They do not need to be planted very deeply, half-inch to one inch at most. I like to create a solid barrier, so I plant my cloves about a half-inch apart. One critical aspect of garlic growing is to remove the long, flowering "scape" when you see it develop in spring. This enables the plant to put all of its energy into bulb production rather than flowering and setting seed.

Every clove you plant will develop into a bulb over the season, providing ample access to homegrown organic garlic. With low water and fertility needs, this just may be the most practical food crop to grow at home.

Garlic
(Allium sativum)
As one of my all-time favorite edibles to grow, garlic belongs along the edge of every sunny landscape because it is a great plant to help deter in-ground pests such as voles and moles, while creating an effective barrier through its foliage for deer, rabbits and groundhogs.

Considering 90% of the garlic sold in American grocery stores is imported from China, this popular culinary bulb has some serious food miles attached to it. It is easy to grow with very little maintenance and can be contained to the edge along any sunny border.

Potatoes
(Solanum tuberosum)
Every kid loves French fries, so why not teach them where their favorite food starts? Potatoes are a very low-maintenance crop that can produce an abundance of edible tubers through the cool season. Since it is in the *Solanaceae* family, the foliage is poisonous and browsing mammals steer clear.

I grow my 'taters the old-fashioned way, in the ground. But I start in my pantry: As my potatoes begin to sprout inside, I cut the growing eyes off in chunks and allow the pieces to dry for several days before planting. Dig a trench 18-24 inches

The potato foliage helps to protect the kale from passing bunnies and deer.

deep around your landscape borders and toss in those vegetative "cuttings," dropping a piece every eight inches. Cover the trench, walk away and three to four months later it will be time to harvest. The foliage will turn yellow, signaling that it is time to dig. You can easily grow large quantities of potatoes along a landscape edge. I leave the smallest tubers in the ground, ensuring the next season's harvest and I am never without homegrown, organically-raised potatoes.

Post-harvest, I store the unwashed potatoes in brown bags inside my pantry for several weeks before starting to cook them. This allows the sugars to settle into starch.

Did you know... a wide-tined garden fork is the best way to harvest potatoes? This will reduce the number of tubers that get stabbed, which causes rapid decay.

Plant a warm season edge
Basil
(Ocimum basilicum)

One of the most recognizable and commonly-grown herbs, basil is a summer staple for gardeners. But animals do not fancy it and are particularly averse to the flavored basil varieties such as lemon-lime, which are ideal for planting in high traffic deer zones. The small leaf forms such as 'Micrette' are excellent candidates to grow along a bed edge, providing a boxwood-like formal appearance, combined with bitter foliage that smells like burning hair! No, this is not your pesto-making basil. Needless to say, this is a highly effective deterrent. You can sow the seed in containers and transplant or, like me, just dig a one-inch trench along the edge and scatter the seed directly.

'Micrette' is my favorite basil for planting along edges.

Peppers
(*Capsicum* sp.)

Like its cousin the potato, peppers are also a solanaceous plant noted for their poisonous foliage (a member of the nightshade family, *Solanaceae*). Peppers love heat and will fruit abundantly as the days become shorter. Requiring much less water and fertilizer compared to other summer crops, dwarf and ornamental peppers are practical to grow along a bed edge.

Peppers are all the rage these days, especially with enthusiasts who like to test their limits for heat tolerance! I prefer to grow easy-to-eat peppers like bell selections, jalapeños, serrano and marconi. Peppers can be slow to germinate from seed, so direct sowing is not recommended. Instead, start your favorite peppers indoors and transplant. Like most warm season crops, they will "sulk" in cool garden soil, so wait to plant until the night temperatures become consistently above 50°F. ■

Planting peppers along the edge also makes harvesting easy.

PART FOUR

what's your pleasure?

Ten

Bringing the Beauty Indoors
Decorating with Grains

*P*erhaps my favorite aspect of being a grain grower is the decorative use of the dried seed heads. My adoration seems to be boundless. You will find a wide variety of cereals on display in my home year-round, especially wheat, barley, oats and sorghum. Of course, rice and corn make seasonal appearances in the autumn.

There are so many ways that you can embellish with grains, both freshly-cut as green seed heads, and fully mature, dried specimens. From wreaths hung on your door to vases on your dining room table, grain arrangements offer natural elegance. I love to make bouquets to share with friends and family and will often add a single stalk to a wrapped package for a unique touch. The versatility of grains is really what makes them practical as a decorative addition, while providing a touch of homegrown, rustic beauty.

I love to incorporate grains into holiday décor. From spring Easter celebrations to summer picnics, grains arrangements offer a unique and unexpected addition to any celebration! And always appropriate for a table setting. You can create a cornucopia-like display using your homegrown harvests for Thanksgiving. And, to make your Christmas tree a standout, consider crafting a grain topper in the shape of a star.

Though I love cut flowers, dried grains are so low maintenance! There is no shedding of petals or pollen and no water to change out. However, I often mix my dried grains with fresh-cut arrangements, to add extra flare and interest.

Moth prevention for indoor arrangements: As sublime as these arrangements can be, you should be alert to a certain six-legged flying pest that can ruin the experience: the Indian meal moth, aka, the pantry moth. (See page 148 for grain storage and general moth-prevention tips.) When I plan to use grains for indoor arrangements, I soak them in a strong bleach solution, to ensure that the Indian-meal moth eggs or larvae will die. This practice also brightens the seed heads. I recommend using a lemon or lavender-scented bleach so your grains will smell nice.

Other things you can do: Freeze your arrangements for a week to kill off any possible life forms, or dry them in your oven on a low temperature, 120°F. Some sources recommend that you microwave the grains, though I think that is more practical for harvests that are bound for consumption rather than for arranging. ■

Eleven

Harvesting and Processing Your Homegrown Grains

*I*f growing grains is the game, harvesting and processing them into an edible form is the trophy. Actually, for a grain-growing gardener it's the equivalent of winning the World Series or Super Bowl.

There are plenty of reasons to grow grains besides eating them. But if you are anything like me, you are probably curious about what to do with these food crops when their season comes to an end.

I am not going to sugar coat it – this is the hard part! The ease of growing the grains gives you the confidence to go through the harvesting and processing. It only takes one time before you develop a deep appreciation for mechanization. I literally dream of having access to a small combine of sorts to make this experience fast and efficient. Alas, that is not the reality for home grain growers at the moment.

Some crops are more complicated than others, since the harvesting and processing approach relates to the seasonality of the grain. For instance, all three of the cool season grains highlighted in this book follow the same general instructions. However, the three warm season selections vary in technique and resources, so I will treat them individually.

Before we get ahead of ourselves, we need to cover some basic harvesting and processing definitions. This will make the explanations clearer and will enable you to sound like an expert.

Awn – a stiff bristle growing from the flower or ear of cereal grasses like wheat, barley and others

Chaff – the hulls of the seed, often paper-like

Ear – the part of a corn plant containing the corncob, husk and kernels

Harvest – the process of gathering a ripe crop

Husk – the leaf-like layer on the outside of corn ears, also known as a "shuck"

Kernel – the seed of a grain plant

Milling – the process in which a grain is ground, often referred to as grinding

Reaping – the cutting of a grain for harvest

Scythe – a blade with a long handle used to cut grass, grain and other crops

Seed head – a flower head in seed

Thresh – to beat out a grain or seed from a stalk by treading, rubbing or striking with a flail, or with a machine

Winnow – to blow away the chaff, leaving just the seed

Yield – the amount of a crop produced in a given time or from a given place

PEST ALERT

There is one major pest consideration related to storing your harvested grains: the Indian-meal moth *(Plodia interpunctella)*, often called pantry moths. I experienced by first infestation a few years ago, when a population hatched on some decorative grains I had brought into the house and made into home décor arrangements. I haven't had problems with my consumable cereals because I keep them frozen – both as raw seed and ground flour. That is really the only way to ensure that you won't have a population develop and spoil your harvest.

If you store grain at room temperature, the larvae of the Indian-meal moth can chew through plastic and cardboard. That is why proper storage is so important. If you have an outbreak, discard the grains immediately. All of the life stages – eggs, larvae and adult – are sensitive to temperature extremes (they can be killed with a week of freezing or a brief heating in the microwave or oven). Eradication can be difficult and time consuming, as these tiny moths can travel throughout your house and tend to hang out around your ceiling and spin cocoons. You can scrub infested areas with soap and water. I have found they are sensitive to rubbing alcohol, which I keep in a spray bottle. Vacuuming the moths was the most efficient way to get them 100% out of my house.

Cool Season Grains

Harvesting and processing cool season grains is intense. Everything ripens at one time, so you are left with a major task of doing it all at once. That is one way they differ from the warm season grains, which ripen over a longer period of time or can be planted in small quantities over a period of several weeks to space out the harvest times.

However, I have come to love the harvesting aspect of my cool season grain crops because it has provided me a unique opportunity to share the experience with others. From my adult friends to school groups, I invite anyone with a passing interest to take part in our hand-harvesting extravaganza – all hands on deck, all at once!

Cultivating a Team

Initially, I took on the job of hand-harvesting alone. It took me a full week. I quickly realized that if I wanted to continue growing grains I had to include more people. In year two, we threw a cocktail harvest party, which was great in theory and resulted in a stellar turnout of participants! However, adults are basically worthless after their second gin and tonic. Even with 20 people – that's 40 hands – we didn't get the full 850-square-foot bed harvested. Determined to figure out a solution for year three, I started thinking outside of our social norms.

LET'S HEAR IT FOR SMALL HANDS: In recent years, I have become a major advocate for child labor. Before you get offended, I don't mean the kind of work that would concern government agencies or a child welfare advocate. Rather, just the simple idea of getting kids OUTSIDE! Allowing them to get their hands dirty and providing them the chance to learn from the environment. Any moment when a child is not looking at a screen is critical. So why not get every child that you know excited about the food they eat by teaching them the art of growing, while using their energy to hand-harvest some grains?

It is a win-win, really. Kids are sponges, and if we want the next generation to become stewards of the land, it is critical that we focus on prioritizing outdoor education. I have been so fortunate to have two of the best gardener helpers in the world living next to me through my entire grain-growing journey. In fact, it was their genuine enthusiasm and interest that has fueled my curiosity year after year. Without Aidan and Abby assisting me with the daily garden tasks, reminding me of all the things I forget and encouraging me to keep pushing the limits, I would never have become the gardener that I am. Even on the hottest days I can count on them to lend a hand.

KIDS AND FOOD, A NATURAL PAIRING: Because of my experience gardening with Aidan and Abby, I developed an interest in elementary school garden outreach. Over the years, I have been fortunate to be involved in many different school programs, all centered around one thing: putting kids to work! Turns out, this digital generation loves to get dirty, chase insects and harvest food just as much as I did as a child. The difference is, they aren't granted the opportunity to explore outside in the same way that we did 40 years ago. That reality is a driving force for me to reach as many children as possible. I want to get them excited about growing food and learning to make better nutritional decisions while feeling empowered as a land steward. There is no room for entitlement anymore. Our environment is fragile and we must train the next generation to do better for a sustainable future.

It is an easy sell to get children excited about growing bread. From seed sowing to harvest, the entire experience is exceptional. Selfishly, I love to have school groups come for the harvest of my cool season grains that grow to only a few feet tall, because they don't have to bend over to reach them. As an adult, albeit a short one at only five foot three inches, I know all too well that hand-harvesting a crop that requires you to bend, even the slightest, can make you resent the process. Kids are the perfect size and their high energy allows them to clear a plot in no time! Make sure you provide ample hydration and fun breaks – like bubble blowing and sidewalk chalk art – so you capture their attention and keep them motivated!

Now I have various organizations who request coming for the grain harvest each year, including Junior Master Gardeners, home school groups and my alma mater, 4-H. This outreach extends my purpose as a home grower while making easy work of a task that at one time seemed insurmountable. I am so grateful for the opportunity to use my little plot of land as a teaching tool for children and adults alike. Truly, the hobby of gardening can change the world for the better.

Harvesting Smart

The way we harvest barley, oats and wheat is quite simple and it doesn't require any scary tools like a scythe or sickle – which probably should not be given to small children anyway! We lay out a tarp or have large buckets stationed in easy throwing distance. Then we move across the planted area and snap the seed head off, leaving the stalk. This approach makes it very fast and clean – no soil flying in the air to contaminate the harvest. Remember, those roots should be left in the ground to rot in place to improve your soil.

Once we have harvested all of the seed heads, we can relocate to a shady spot for the rest of the processing. I do recommend harvesting in the early morning and evening when the temperatures are pleasant, especially if you live in a region that is hot and humid. Since you have grown your grains in full sun, harvesting in the midday heat is not wise. Always think about how to make a task as pleasant as possible; working in sweltering heat is a quick way to make you hate the garden.

Threshing and Winnowing

This is where mechanization really helps, and frankly I am not sure how to do this without the home-engineered tool that my husband crafted. I wish I could recommend an all-in-one cultivator, but I have yet to find one that is logical for small-batch growers.

We use a 5-gallon bucket with a lid, an electric drill and a long rod with chain link attached to it. There is a hole in the lid that allows for the rod to fit through. The idea is simple: Fill the bucket halfway with the seed heads, and then beat them to oblivion with the fast-spinning pieces of metal. By the time you finish, the contents of the bucket will be unrecognizable.

The next step is to winnow. This is the part that everyone enjoys. Using a fan – ideally a box fan or industrial fan – you will slowly pour the beaten mixture from the 5-gallon bucket into a large-mouth container, like a Rubbermaid storage bin, while the fan is blowing. Eventually, you will blow away all of the chaff and what will remain is the seed, because it is heavy and cannot float away.

SOME GOOD ADVICE, FROM HAVING DONE THIS THE `WRONG WAY`: Set up your winnowing station in an area where you can blow the chaff into a garden bed. It is an excellent addition of organic matter for soil improvement.

Threshing and winnowing is a process – it may take ten more times of repeating it before you get to raw, clean seed. Don't lose faith; it doesn't have to get done all at once! You can store seed heads under shelter for several weeks, but make sure they have adequate airflow, or they will rot. It is also important to check for rodents and "wildlife" that will sneak in and steal your grain! Birds are notorious for scavenging from my grain piles.

Once you have clean seed, you can grind it into flour (see "Milling Your Grain" on page 158) or you can store it for next season's sowing. Either way, keep it in the refrigerator or freezer. This is whole-grain, unbleached seed and it will spoil if left outdoors through the heat of the summer. You can find delicious recipes for your hard-won grains in Chapter 12.

With the harvest finished, you can now turn your attention to preparing the bed for the next season. By harvesting just the seed heads of your cool season grains, you will still have the remaining stalks standing. Instead of cutting them down, or worse, pulling them out, mow that biomass back in place! Using a gas or electric push mower, you can chop these stalks down and they will quickly decompose, enriching your soil for the next season's crop.

Warm Season Grains

Harvesting warm season grains is fun, with each crop having its own unique approach. Unlike the cool season grains that all get harvested at one time using the same technique, these summer growers will each be harvested at different times for varied edible purposes. For instance, fresh-eating corn is harvested in the middle of the growing season, whereas rice and grain sorghum won't be harvested until they dry out. For that reason, I have created individual harvesting and processing descriptions for each of the warm season grains. (For how to grind these grains into flour, see "Milling Your Grain" on page 158.)

CORN

Of all the grains, both cool and warm season, corn is the most reliable producer, notably for fresh eating.

SWEET CORN: Harvesting corn on the cob is likely the most intuitive for home gardeners, as it is more like picking a fresh tomato or pepper. Peeling back the husk and removing the silk is likely something that everyone has done at least once in your life. The best advice is to start checking the ears three weeks after the silks first appear. Another way to see if your sweet corn is ready for picking is to cut a kernel open. If white juice drips, it is time! I have been known to enjoy a raw cob as soon as it was picked. Honestly, there is nothing better than fresh, homegrown corn on the cob.

Dried corn, ready for grinding into grits.

POPCORN, ETC.: Other varieties of corn, such as the dent selection of 'Bloody Butcher' and popcorn, are meant to stay on the stalk until the plant dries out. My baseline for this is quite simple: When the plants are too ugly to remain, that is when I harvest. I first remove the dried ears and then cut the corn stalks to use for fall decoration, leaving the roots to rot in place. When the autumn decor is over I lay the stalks on the grass and mow them, allowing the clippings to blow back into the landscape bed. I husk the dried ears, removing the outer paper-like leaves and cleaning the cob of dried silk. Then, over a bucket, I begin to twist the cob in my hands to encourage the kernels to pop off. Once you get it started, the dried seeds are easy to remove.

At this stage it is ready to be stored or eaten – either popped or ground into corn grits or meal. I store my whole kernels in a large, well-sealed jar placed in my pantry. The ground corn is best vacuum-sealed and frozen for future use.

RICE

Harvesting your own homegrown rice is probably one of the most authentic experiences you can have as a gardener. Perhaps "authentic" is another word for time consuming, but I swear it is worth a try.

Rice should be harvested once the seeds appear to be brown and dry. Cut the seed heads off from the stem, leaving the foliage. That will make excellent compost! Once you have harvested all the ripe seed heads, it is time to thresh and winnow – just like the cool season grains. In fact, I use the same threshing setup: 5-gallon bucket with the drill adapted to beat the chaff off the seed. Following a thorough threshing, I winnow using a box fan, allowing the chaff to blow into a nearby landscape bed. As I dump the bucket, the grain seeds will fall straight down into the container. You will likely need to repeat the threshing and winnowing process several times to ensure the seed is fully removed from any existing plant material.

Did you know... rice has to be de-hulled before it is milled? It differs from wheat, which is ready for milling after threshing and winnowing.

DE-HULLING: This can be achieved by rubbing the seeds between your hands. I will warn you, this is not the most enjoyable. If you are a serious home rice grower, investing in a professional rice huller is a good idea. These devices are somewhat difficult to source and can cost upwards of $500, which is why I haven't taken the plunge. Instead, I choose to do small batches by hand for eating, but primarily grow my rice for its ornamental qualities.

Milling is a crucial step in making rice edible. If you only remove the hull (husk), the result is brown rice. If you further mill or polish the seed, removing the bran layer, you will achieve white rice. I store my milled rice in the freezer to ensure that it will not spoil, and when I indulge in my homegrown harvest I have an added appreciation for the easy accessibility we enjoy thanks to the global food marketplace.

I think it is totally fair to grow rice just because it is pretty. Obviously, it requires time to harvest and process, and I am the first to acknowledge that time is not always a luxury we have. Most of the time I harvest my rice seed and just stash it away in the refrigerator for planting the following year. No matter what you intend to do with your rice crop, it is still a fun plant to grow!

This rice is not yet ready for harvest.

SORGHUM

There are several uses for sorghum, including the seeds and the sugary sap (as I mentioned in the earlier description, page 99). Harvesting the grain is easier than crushing the canes, but I encourage you to do both – at least one time. Both the seeds and the canes will be ripe for harvesting in mid-fall, though the canes are best harvested before the seeds are fully mature.

GRAIN SORGHUM: The hard seeds from grain sorghum can be harvested in fall when the plant begins to dry out. Just cut the seed head from the stalk and place in a warm, well-ventilated area for about a week to dry thoroughly. I hang bunches of seed heads from the rafters of a covered porch. The final step is to roll the dried seeds over a screen or sieve to remove any chaff. You can thresh and winnow as you would with wheat, if you prefer, but sorghum seed is much cleaner and doesn't really require that much effort. I recommend storing your seed in the freezer and cooking them within nine months.

The seed can also be milled into a gluten-free flour for baked goods, breads and pastas, or used for brewing beer or other spirits. And of course, the birds favor sorghum seed, so even if you aren't planning to eat it, you can provide nourishment for local wildlife.

CANE SORGHUM: This is a totally different process, which involves harvesting the full cane. I confessed in my earlier commentary that I have yet to be successful in this method, but I have not lost faith. One of my local friends and a fellow gardening enthusiast has invested

Sorghum seed can be harvested to eat, replant, or used to feed the birds.

in a real cane mill, so this fall I plan to haul my harvests and use his equipment, in addition to trying out my new hand crank press. I have a feeling the mechanized option is going to be the winner!

There is actually a sorghum festival held in the North Carolina mountains, where you can watch as a horse walks round and round, powering the press. You can also sample the sweet, green goodness. The process isn't terribly complicated and it begins by cutting the canes at ground level two weeks after the "milk stage"; that is just a reference to the immature seed, which at this stage will ooze a white liquid when pierced. However, you can eat the immature seed by cooking it, much as you would pasta.

Remove the leaves before you guide the cane into the press. Be sure to have a large bucket or container underneath to collect the light-green juice that will drip from the extraction process. The final step is to boil the juice down to syrup, which used to be done in caldrons over pit fires. Instead, I recommend using your outdoor grill, just in case you make a mess. This sugary goodness is sticky!

Did you know... sorghum syrup is actually sweeter than traditional molasses? It can be added to any recipe calling for molasses or honey.

As you would with honey, store sorghum syrup at room temperature in darkness – like in your pantry. If it begins to crystallize, you can put the bottle in a bowl of warm water or just heat it in the microwave for about ten seconds. It can be added to tea and even used for baked goods. The main reason I became interested in growing cane sorghum was to provide my own sugar for my candied jalapeño peppers. I am hopeful that this will be the season for the dream to become a reality!

Milling Your Grain

There are many ways to grind your grains into flour – from a mortar and pestle to hand crank and electric mills. You will find an endless supply through online retailers. I started by using a hand crank grinder, and it was a great workout!

But the texture was very coarse, so over the years I have upgraded my equipment.

The two electric mills I use are the Wonder Mill and the KitchenAid All Metal Grain Mill attachment. Both work great for any of the grains I grow. The main difference is the quantity. If I need to grind several cups of flour, the Wonder Mill is the better choice.

Did you know... 1 cup of grain seed, such as wheat, produces 1¾ cups of flour?

It is best to only grind as much flour as you plan to use. Freshly ground whole grains can spoil quickly. You can mill any cereal grain into flour, though wheat is the most common. (Rice flour is commonly used when making Asian-inspired dishes and corn grits are a favorite of mine!)

ROLLED OATS: If you have harvested enough oats to use in the kitchen, a feat I have yet to achieve, you can roll your own oats for oatmeal and baking purposes.

When rolling oats at home, you will find they will look different from the commercially processed choices, which are steamed and flattened. Home-rolled oats will retain their seed shape, but will be thinner because of your rolling. A "grain flaker" is a device that will essentially flatten the grain for you. There are electric and manual options, including an attachment for a KitchenAid mixer.

(See the Resources [page 187] for mills information.) ■

Twelve

Recipes

Cooking with your homegrown grains is probably the most unique and memorable yard-to-table experience you will have. Unlike other more common home garden crops like peppers and tomatoes, grains require an extra bit of attention in order to be used in the kitchen. But if you follow the prep instructions in Chapter 10 you will be ready to try any of these recipes!

I believe it is important to emphasize the experiencing of growing AND eating your own food. Sure, it is easy to go to the store and buy everything pre-made. But there is an undeniable satisfaction to actually being a part of your food chain. Of course, it is unrealistic to think that everyone is going to go back to the days of cooking from scratch. But perhaps it isn't so crazy to consider that people cook at least one time in their life from raw, homegrown ingredients. That is my goal, simply to encourage people to experience the phenomenon of "yard to table" eating at least one time.

Thanks to my dear friend and professional pastry chef Justin Dillree, I have been able to adapt many recipes from online sources like allrecipes.com and others. With his oversight, we have created delicious, easy-to-make recipes using homegrown grains as inspiration.

MEET CHEF JUSTIN

"In my youth I was surrounded by vast fields of wheat, oats, safflower, corn and barley. My earliest culinary memories are with my mother and grandmother, baking dinner rolls for family gatherings. I had so much fun learning from them and absorbing the creative love that went into every moment. Through the development of my culinary career I have been driven by passion and love for everything I make, always wanting to learn and grow. Baking is where my heart ultimately took me, with a focus on both sweet and savory breads and pastries. I love to try new grains and flours, each revealing a new flavor, texture, and story. I am grateful for the fun-loving recipes that I have been able to learn and share while collaborating with Brie on this project."

Chef Justin earned a Culinary Arts degree from Wake Technical Community College, with a focus on baking and pastry. He has worked at highly regarded restaurants and bakeries in the Southeast, including the Michelin-rated One in Chapel Hill.

You may notice that some of these recipes are a bit indulgent. Yes, I like to add bacon, butter and cheese to my recipes. At my house we call that combination "culinary duct tape." That combination of ingredients is basically guaranteed to make any meal taste better. Remember, everything in moderation and we all deserve to indulge now and again. Also, if you are growing these grains and hand harvesting and processing you may deserve a few extra calories after a hard day of threshing!

Even if you don't grow enough to cook, all of these grains can easily be found at grocery stores such as Aldi and Whole Foods. These recipes can be converted for specific dietary restrictions as well. I encourage you to try them, adjust them to your liking and share the results with your loved ones.

BARLEY | Vegetarian Barley Greek Salad

Preparation time: 15 minutes • Cook time: 45 minutes • 4 servings

This simple whole-grain salad made with barley and garden fresh vegetables is a delicious way to impress your friends and family with your homegrown harvest. The vinegar-based dressing adds a tangy, refreshing flavor. You can omit the cheese, feta and chicken breast to make this dish vegetarian or vegan. I like to add extra cucumber, peppers and tomatoes when they are abundant in my garden.

Served warm or chilled, this recipe has become a staple in our house, especially for entertaining. It is easy to increase the quantities to feed more than a dozen.

INGREDIENTS

3 cups water

½ teaspoon salt

1 cup pearl barley

¼ cup olive oil

2 tablespoons balsamic vinegar (or red wine vinegar)

5 marinated artichoke hearts

1 cucumber, chopped

1 red onion, chopped

3 sweet peppers, chopped

10 cherry tomatoes, halved

¼ cup Kalamata olives, pitted, chopped

¼ cup fresh parsley or mint, finely chopped

½ teaspoon oregano

Pinch of salt, to taste

½ cup crumbled feta

1 chicken breast, grilled

Drizzle of glazed balsamic vinegar

DIRECTIONS

- Bring water to a boil and add the half-teaspoon of salt. Add barley, cover, and allow to simmer over medium-low heat for about 40 minutes, or until barley is cooked. Drain excess water into a colander and rinse the cooked barley with cold water. Place in large bowl and set aside.

- Whisk together the olive oil and balsamic vinegar and gently toss with the barley to coat well

- Allow the barley to cool slightly and add the artichoke hearts, cucumber, onion, peppers, tomatoes, olives, fresh mint and oregano.

- Plate and add sliced grilled chicken breast and crumbled feta overtop.

- Drizzle glazed balsamic vinegar around edges as a delicious accent. Glazed balsamic vinegar is available at most grocery stores, but it is easy to make at home. To glaze: Mix 2 cups of balsamic vinegar with ½ cup brown sugar in a saucepan. Stirring constantly, cook over medium heat until the sugar fully dissolves. Simmer on low for about 20 minutes, until the vinegar is reduced by half. Glaze should be sticky and thick. Extra glaze can be stored in the refrigerator. Be sure to use a jar with a tight lid – I like to make 1-pint jars for regular use.

BARLEY | Beef and Barley

Preparation time: 30 minutes • Cook time: 6 hours • 8 servings

Beef and Barley is a classic winter comfort food. This is a simple and delicious way to use your home-grown or store-bought barley. Your family and friends will be thrilled when you serve this on a cold evening and you will have very little cleanup at the end of the meal. You are basically only using one cooking vessel.

There are several ways you can make this recipe, which will result in different finished dishes. As a soup, I have used a slow cooker, which is easy and creates a traditional soup consistency. If you prefer thick broth, make a roux by melting butter and adding an equal part of flour. Once the flour and butter are well incorporated, add the thin broth and whisk vigorously. That will create a more stew-like consistency.

But my new favorite method for preparing Beef and Barley is to bake it in a 400°F oven in a cast iron pot for 2½ hours. This will result in a delicious, broth-free rendition more like a risotto or a casserole, which can be served on plates rather than as a soup in bowls. Both approaches result in a comforting, nutritious meal, so you really can't go wrong.

INGREDIENTS

1 stick salted butter

1 three-pound beef roast (cooked whole in slow cooker or chopped into cubes for oven baking)

Salt and ground pepper, to taste

6-8 cups water (depending on how much broth you desire)

Equal parts flour and butter (optional, for roux)

1 cup barley

3 carrots, chopped

3 stalks celery, chopped

1 garlic bulb, chopped

1 onion, chopped

2 sweet peppers, chopped

2 tablespoons sage

DIRECTIONS FOR BEEF AND BARLEY SOUP IN A SLOW COOKER

- Melt butter in a large skillet over medium heat. Gently wash the roast, then place in skillet to sear, about 2 minutes each side.

- Lightly sprinkle salt and pepper on all sides. Place roast into slow cooker with 6-8 cups of water. Note: If you desire a thicker broth, prepare and mix the roux with the water before adding the roast.

- Cover the roast with the extra butter from skillet and cook on high for 4-5 hours or until the meat easily falls apart. Add barley, carrots, celery, garlic, onion, peppers and sage during the last hour of cooking.

- Serve in bowls. Add salt and pepper to taste.

DIRECTIONS FOR BEEF AND BARLEY CASSEROLE BAKED IN A CAST IRON POT IN THE OVEN

- Preheat oven to 400°F

- Melt butter in a large skillet over medium heat.

- Gently wash the roast and cube the meat. Place beef cubes into skillet to sear. Lightly sprinkle salt and pepper. Stir beef cubes for about 3 minutes, ensuring all sides are seared.

- Add the seared cubes and butter to a cast iron pot. Add 6-8 cups of water. Cover with lid and place in center of preheated oven.

- Cook the roast for 3 hours (until the meat easily falls apart). Add barley, carrots, celery, garlic, onion, peppers and sage during the last hour of cooking.

- Remove from oven and allow to cool for 15 minutes with lid off.

- Serve on plates. Drizzle your choice of condiments, like sriracha or glazed balsamic vinegar and add salt and pepper to taste.

CORN | Spicy Rainbow Grits

Preparation time: 20 minutes • Cook time: 40 minutes • 4 Servings

Grits were not something I ever had as a child, but when I moved to North Carolina that changed. Trust me when I say, not all grits are created equal. After eating these, you will never order fast-food grits again. If you have never had really good grits, this is your chance! This easy recipe will add spice to your life. You can grind your own or simply buy them at the grocery store. Add your favorite cheese, adjust the spice level for your liking – I add three dried whole peppers to amp up the heat. Top with crumbled bacon and you have a hearty meal that can be served any time of day.

INGREDIENTS

2 cups whole milk

2 cups water

1 tablespoon sea salt and freshly ground black pepper

1 cup grits

4 slices bacon (optional garnish)

1 tablespoon olive oil

1 jalapeño pepper, cored and sliced into rings

1 medium sweet onion, diced

2 tablespoons unsalted butter

1 cup cubed aged sharp Cheddar cheese

INSTRUCTIONS

- Preheat oven to 350°F
- In a medium pot add milk, water and 1 teaspoon salt. Turn to high heat and boil.
- Gradually whisk in the grits (if you add them all at once they will clump). Turn heat to low and simmer for 30 minutes, stirring frequently (if they stick they will scorch)
- Place bacon slices on a rack and bake until crispy, usually 20 minutes. Remove from oven, pat dry and crumble.
- During the last 10 minutes of cooking the grits, heat a saucepan over medium-high heat. Add olive oil, sliced jalapeño and chopped onion and sauté, stirring frequently for 3 minutes
- Stir butter and cheese into the grits, making sure they melt evenly. You can serve the sautéed jalapeño and onions as a topper or mix them in for a full flavor combination. Either way, they are delicious!
- Sprinkle bacon as desired. Add salt and pepper to taste.

CORN | Garlic Creamed Corn

Preparation time: 10 minutes • Cook time: 15 minutes • 4 servings

Originating with the Native American culture, creamed corn is a delicious side for meals served throughout the year, but especially when corn is in season. This is a great recipe using fresh corn on the cob, but frozen corn can be substituted in a pinch. With only five ingredients, this is simple enough to teach anyone, especially kids. This is comfort food at its best!

INGREDIENTS

4 ears corn

¾ cup heavy cream

1 tablespoon butter

3 cloves garlic, sliced

1 teaspoon salt

1 teaspoon sugar

DIRECTIONS

- Wash and shuck the corncobs, removing all silk.
- Cut the kernels from the cob, then scrape the cobs with the edge of a knife to squeeze the "corn milk" out of the cob.
- In a large saucepan, bring cream, butter, corn, garlic, salt and sugar to a boil. Reduce heat and simmer uncovered for 15 minutes.
- Add salt and pepper to taste.

OATS | Traditional Oatmeal

Preparation time: 5 minutes • Cook time: 10 minutes • 2 servings

Note: The following oat recipes call for rolled oats. If you are using your garden-grown oats, see milling tips on page 158.

This tried-and-true recipe for a breakfast staple is an easy way to make the most of your oatmeal harvest or just use store-bought oats like I do. With simple ingredients, easy directions, protein and fiber, this is a perfect way to start your day. Add nuts, fresh fruit or my favorite, peanut butter, to make it a meal customized to every member of your family.

INGREDIENTS

1 cup rolled oats

1 cup milk

¼ teaspoon sea salt

1 teaspoon brown sugar

1 cup water

1 tablespoon honey

½ teaspoon cinnamon

½ cup desired toppings

DIRECTIONS

- Combine oats, milk, salt, sugar and water in a medium saucepan. Bring to a boil and reduce to low heat.

- Simmer uncovered for 10 minutes until thick, stirring occasionally. Remove from heat and let cool slightly.

- Divide equally between two bowls. Drizzle each serving with honey and sprinkle with cinnamon. Add desired toppings and serve warm.

OATS | Chocolate Chip Oatmeal Ice Cream Sandwiches

Preparation time: 20 minutes • Cook time: 10 minutes • 12 servings

Chocolate chip oatmeal cookies are a tasty treat for people of every age. Add growing, harvesting and milling your own oats and suddenly ordinary cookies become very special. So gather up your favorite children and make a batch of cookies and some lifelong memories!

The idea to make these into ice cream sandwiches took this to a next-level dessert – a simple way to turn an ordinary thing like a cookie into something unforgettable. You can use store-bought whipped cream or easily make it from scratch by mixing 1 cup of chilled heavy whipping cream with 2-3 tablespoons of powdered sugar. Beat until it begins to fluff – usually 1-2 minutes in my KitchenAid.

INGREDIENTS

1 cup butter, softened

1 cup white sugar

1 cup packed brown sugar

2 eggs

1 teaspoon vanilla extract

2 cups all-purpose flour

1 teaspoon baking soda

1 teaspoon salt

1½ teaspoons ground cinnamon

½ cup chocolate chips

3 cups rolled oats

1 container Talenti® Vanilla Gelato (or similar quality)

1 cup whipped topping

Dash cinnamon sugar

DIRECTIONS

- In a medium bowl, mix together butter, white sugar and brown sugar. Beat in eggs and stir in vanilla.

- In a separate bowl combine dry ingredients (flour, baking soda, salt and cinnamon) and stir into the creamed mixture.

- Add the oats and chocolate chips, incorporating them fully. Cover and chill dough for at least 1 hour.

- Preheat oven to 375°F.

- Line baking sheets with a non-stick silicone mat or parchment.

- Pinch apart small amounts of dough and form into balls about the size of a walnut. Space 2 inches apart on cookie sheets. Flatten with a large fork or use your thumb – your hands are dough-y already!

- Bake for 8-10 minutes. Allow cookies to cool on baking sheets for 5 minutes before transferring to a wire rack. Allow cookies to cool completely.

TO ASSEMBLE

- Place one cookie on a small plate with the flat side facing up. Scoop vanilla gelato onto center and flatten edges with a spoon. Add another cookie on top.

- Finish with a scoop of whipped topping and a sprinkle of cinnamon sugar. Serve with an extra napkin, as these can be messy.

RICE | Spanish Rice

Preparation: 15 minutes • Cook time: 30 minutes • 5 servings

Spanish rice is a staple in our house and has become our go-to meal for large dinner parties. Best thing, it is easy to convert to a vegetarian or vegan dish. You can add seasonal vegetables and various proteins including beef, chicken or shrimp to change it up. You can serve it with tortilla chips as an appetizer or use as the main course. The versatility of this dish makes it a recipe that will work for any occasion, no matter the crowd.

Of course, when you tell the story of this recipe you must begin with the day you sowed the rice seed. That is an authentic way to start off a dinner conversation! But, even if you don't use the rice you grew, this recipe will work well with store-bought white or brown rice, just be sure to adjust cook times to reflect the rice you are using.

INGREDIENTS

8 slices bacon

½ stick salted butter

1 cup uncooked rice

2 cups water

1 garlic blub, minced

1 sweet onion, diced

1 jalapeño pepper, sliced with seed
    (remove seed if desired)

2 sweet peppers, sliced

1 tomato, diced

1 tablespoon salt

1 tablespoon ground pepper

1 tablespoon cumin

¼ cup shredded cheese

1 avocado

1 bunch cilantro, chopped

1 lime (cut into wedges)

Drizzle of olive oil

DIRECTIONS

- Preheat oven to 350°F

- Place bacon slices on a cookie sheet on a rack and bake until crisp, about 20 minutes. Remove from oven, pat dry with paper towels and allow to cool.

- Melt butter in a large skillet over medium heat. Mix rice into skillet, stirring often. When rice begins to brown, stir in water and bring to a boil.

- Add garlic, onions, peppers, tomato, salt, pepper and cumin. Reduce heat, cover and simmer for 20 minutes or until the liquid has been absorbed and the rice is fully cooked. (This will take 40 minutes for traditional brown rice).

- Crumble or chop the bacon. Plate the rice and sprinkle cheese and bacon on top. Garnish with avocado slices, cilantro and a lime wedge, and finish with a drizzle of olive oil.

RICE | Vanilla Rice Pudding

Preparation time: 20 minutes • Cook time: 50 minutes • 4 Servings

There are two types of rice pudding, the custard kind that is a baked dessert and this one, the really simple one-pot-and-done version. I do not have much of a sweet tooth, so I prefer this recipe because it goes easy on the sugar. The addition of raisins, cranberries and other dried or fresh fruit, like citrus, adds a nice pop of flavor. I like to finish mine with a dark rum kicker – it is optional but truly does take this dessert to the next level!

INGREDIENTS

2 cups water

2 cups rice

1 teaspoon butter

1 teaspoon salt

1 vanilla bean

1 cup milk

1 tablespoon heavy cream

1 teaspoon cornstarch

2 tablespoons brown sugar

1 tablespoon dark rum

Cinnamon sugar, for dusting

Fresh or dried fruit

Fresh mint garnish

DIRECTIONS

- Bring water to a boil in a saucepan. Stir rice, butter, salt and vanilla bean into water until the butter melts. Cover saucepan, remove from heat and set aside until water is absorbed, about 5 minutes.

- Stir cream, cornstarch and brown sugar into the rice. Bring to a simmer over medium heat while stirring. Cook until the rice has the consistency of loose oatmeal, about 20 minutes.

- In last 5 minutes, add dark rum and stir well.

- Ladle into bowls and dust with cinnamon sugar. Top with fresh or dried fruit (I like to add dried cranberries and fresh orange slices).

- Garnish with fresh mint.

SORGHUM | Tropical Vegan Sorghum Salad

Preparation time: 20 minutes • Cook time: 60 minutes • 6 servings

This is an easy way to make a sorghum dish that will convert even the most skeptical diners. Though not common in the American diet, whole-grain sorghum is prepared just like rice or quinoa by steaming it with water. You can make it on the stovetop, in a slow cooker, in the oven or in a rice cooker. I find it easiest to cook in a small pot on the stove, which is how this recipe was created.

Whole-grain sorghum offers a delicious sweet and nutty flavor and is well complemented by citrus and spicy garden-fresh ingredients like peppers. You can alter this recipe by adding an assortment of your favorite fresh vegetables and seasonings. This sorghum salad recipe is not spicy but does have a great combination of flavors and is vegan. You can add protein or cheese if desired.

I like to cook the sorghum a day in advance and refrigerate overnight. Then I mix the ingredients and serve as a cold salad. It can be a main course or a starter and pairs very well with bubbly wines, such as Champagne or mimosas.

Note: Both forms of sorghum (whole grain and syrup) can be found at Whole Foods across North America and can be purchased from online retailers.

INGREDIENTS

5 cups water

1 cup whole-grain sorghum, uncooked (will make 3 cups cooked)

½ bunch cilantro, chopped

¼ pineapple, chopped

3 sweet peppers, chopped

½ sweet onion, chopped

10 cherry tomatoes cut in half

2-3 tablespoons apple cider vinegar

2-3 tablespoons olive oil

½ lime

1 tablespoon cumin

Salt and pepper, to taste

DIRECTIONS

- In a small saucepan, bring water to a boil. Add the sorghum and cover with a tight-fitting lid. Lower heat to medium and simmer for 1 hour or until tender. Remove from heat and allow to cool. I recommend chilling in the refrigerator for several hours or overnight.

- In a large bowl, combine the chopped cilantro, pineapple, peppers, onion and tomatoes. Add a generous drizzle of apple cider vinegar and olive oil. Squeeze the lime wedge and add cumin. Stir ingredients together well.

- Mix in the chilled sorghum and stir vigorously, ensuring that everything is coated. Refrigerate for 30 minutes to allow flavors to set.

- Season to taste with salt and pepper.

SORGHUM | Ginger, Rum and Sorghum Cookies (GRS cookies)

Preparation time: 20 minutes • Cook time: 30 minutes • Makes 2 dozen cookies

Truth be told, the first time I made these cookies I had very low expectations. I was shocked when I walked into the kitchen while they were baking – it smelled like the holidays. I have never been a gingerbread fan, but these cookies converted me. The sorghum syrup provides a light, sweet flavor and combines perfectly with the ginger spices. The addition of the dark rum adds a depth of flavor and amazing scent while cooking. These cookies are surprisingly easy to make and are sure to be a hit with everyone in your life. Truly, they are the perfect treat to leave for Santa, or anyone else who does nice things for you.

(Note: Some people love cloves; I'm one of those who don't, so I've left cloves out of this recipe. If you must have it, please feel free to add!)

INGREDIENTS

1 ¾ cup flour

1 ½ teaspoon baking soda

½ teaspoon salt

1 teaspoon cinnamon

1 teaspoon ginger

½ teaspoon ground allspice

½ cup (1 stick) unsalted butter, softened

½ cup sorghum syrup

¼ cup granulated sugar

2 tablespoons brown sugar

1 egg

1 teaspoon vanilla extract

1 teaspoon dark rum

¼ cup finely chopped candied ginger

Coarse sugar for rolling

DIRECTIONS

- Preheat oven to 375°F.
- Combine flour, baking soda, salt, cinnamon, ginger and allspice in a small bowl.
- In a larger bowl, beat butter, sorghum syrup and both sugars together until smooth. Mix in egg, vanilla and rum and stir until combined.
- Using a hand or stand mixer, combine the wet and dry ingredients. Mix until the dough is uniform in texture. Refrigerate for at least one hour.
- Line two baking sheets with a silicone mat or parchment paper (to ensure cookies will not stick) and set aside.
- Form the dough into one-inch balls and roll in coarse sugar until fully coated. Place onto cookie sheets at least two inches apart, to allow for expansion.
- Bake for eight-ten minutes, or until the tops of the cookies are golden. Allow to cool for ten minutes before serving.

WHEAT | Beginner's Yeast Bread

Preparation time: 30 minutes • Cook time: 40 minutes • Makes 2 loaves

I must confess, there is a big difference between the flour I mill from my homegrown wheat and the flour you buy at the grocery store. That fluffy, pure white flour we have grown accustomed to seeing is not what you will produce from home. Rather, what you will create is something far more nutritious and full of fiber, and therefore worth eating. It may not be ideal for pastries and bread exclusively, which is why Chef Justin recommended mixing my homegrown flour with store-bought to ensure quality. Typically, I use my homegrown flour for baked goods that are more forgiving than bread, as the texture is rough, which is why the Blueberry Crisp is an ideal starting recipe (page 180). But don't let that stop you from trying this classic bread recipe!

This was the first bread recipe I ever followed and it did not disappoint. Over the years, I have made some changes to adapt the recipe for my taste. It is messy, so be prepared to get your hands sticky through the kneading process. This recipe makes two loaves; my recommendation is to treat yourself to one and freeze the other to avoid the overeating debacle that occurred at my house! Making bread is fun because there are a lot of different steps, so pour a glass of wine and enjoy the process.

INGREDIENTS

1 tablespoon active dry yeast

1 tablespoon sugar

1 tablespoon salt

2 cups warm water (not over 110°F)

3 cups homegrown flour (I prefer emmer or Kamut ground in the Wonder Mill on the bread setting)

3 cups bread flour (my favorite is King Arthur)

Cornmeal or flour for dusting

Boiling water

INSTRUCTIONS

- The mixing process is pretty simple and can be done by hand or in a mixer.
- In a large bowl, stir together the yeast, sugar, salt and warm water. Let that stand until the yeast is completely dissolved.
- Gradually add the flour one cup at a time to the liquid and mix until the dough pulls away from the sides of the bowl.
- Turn the dough out onto a floured surface to begin the kneading process.
- Kneading will cause your bread to be light and fluffy rather than hard and flat, if you do it right! When I first started making bread I didn't knead very well and thus my bread was "thick" (kind of like my waistline!).

- To knead: Start by folding the far edge of the dough over itself and press your palms into it. Press into the dough with the heels of your hands and push away, stretching and compressing the dough. After each pressing, rotate the dough and keep going. As you work, sprinkle more small amounts of flour on the kneading surface to avoid sticking. Stop after about 5 minutes.

- Now it's time to let the dough rise.

- Lightly grease a clean mixing bowl. I use the wrapper from a stick of butter, a tip that Chef Justin shared. Place the dough inside the greased bowl, turning it over once to ensure the top is coated. Cover with a damp towel and set on the counter at room temperature until the dough doubles in size, which will take about 2 hours

- After it has risen, rough up the ball for a minute to shape it and knead out any air bubbles. Cut the dough in half and proceed to forming it into your desired shape. Round or oval are my go-to's.

- Line your cookie sheet with a silicone mat, then sprinkle the mat with a generous amount of cornmeal and place the loaves on the mat. (Even though the silicone mat is non-stick, I still sprinkle the cornmeal...for insurance!) Allow the dough to rest for at least 5 minutes before baking, though it is often recommended to allow your shaped dough to rise for an additional 45 minutes.

- The next step is baking, so get ready to make your house smell amazing.

- Preheat oven to 500°F. On the bottom shelf, place a roasting pan filled halfway with boiling water. This will provide moisture to the loaves while they bake.

- Gently slash the tops of the loaves about ¼-inch deep. On a round loaf I do an X; on an oval I make 3 diagonal cuts. Lightly brush loaves with cold water. Place on the middle rack in the oven and bake for 10 minutes.

- Lower the temperature to 400°F and bake for 10 more minutes. Remove from the oven and allow to cool for 30 minutes on a rack before slicing and serving.

WHEAT | Blueberry Crisp

Preparation time: 15 minutes • Cook time: 45 minutes • 20 servings

I am not much of a baker, but when I started growing my own wheat I decided I needed to try a simple, tasty recipe that I could use my coarsely ground home-grown flour in. My mother-in-law suggested her favorite online recipe source, Smitten Kitchen. Since I also grow blueberries, this recipe for Blueberry Bars seemed practical and easy. Plus, it is a kid-friendly dessert that is perfect for a summer celebration!

This recipe is so perfect that I haven't made any significant adjustments. I do recommend letting it cool, or even chill in the refrigerator overnight, if you are planning to serve it as bars. When served fresh from the oven it crumbles and is best paired with vanilla ice cream and a dab of whipped cream.

INGREDIENTS

1 cup granulated sugar

3 cups all-purpose flour
(or homegrown and hand-ground not-so-fine flour)

1 teaspoon baking powder

¼ teaspoon salt

Fresh zest and juice of 1 lemon

1 cup (2 sticks) cold salted butter

1 egg

½ cup white sugar

4 teaspoons cornstarch

4-6 cups fresh blueberries

DIRECTIONS

- Preheat oven to 375°F and lightly grease a 9x13-inch pan.

- In a medium bowl, stir together the sugar, flour and baking powder. Mix in salt and lemon zest (but not the juice). Add butter and egg and use a pastry cutter or fork to blend until a crumbly consistency.

- Transfer half of the dough to the pan, patting to cover the bottom evenly.

- In another bowl, stir together sugar, cornstarch and lemon juice. Carefully mix in the blueberries, then distribute the fruit over the dough in the pan. Crumble remaining dough over the berry layer.

- Bake for 45 minutes or until top is slightly brown. Allow to fully cool before cutting into squares.

- Best served the next day, after time in the refrigerator.

WHEAT | Wheat Tortillas

Preparation time: 1 hour • Cook time: 2 minutes • Makes 20 tortillas

Homegrown, homemade flour tortillas are my husband, David's, specialty. He will make them for a small dinner party to show off his kitchen skills. The truth is, they are not time consuming or difficult to make, But the flavor difference is remarkable! If you are going to go through the effort of growing, harvesting, threshing and grinding your wheat, you might as well make something delicious from it. Flour tortillas are the base for all my favorite meals, which is why I wanted to share David's adapted recipe with you.

The tortillas are particularly delicious when made from scratch using whole-wheat flour and served warm. You can add your favorite ingredients and use these flour tortillas as a base for tacos, enchiladas, fajitas and quesadillas.

This recipe makes about 20 average-size tortillas; you can freeze the leftovers, if you have any. This is a fun way to impress guests with a zero-food-miles dinner party using your own homegrown flour!

INGREDIENTS

3 cups all-purpose flour

1 teaspoon salt

1 teaspoon baking powder

⅓ cup olive oil

1 cup cold water

DIRECTIONS

- In a bowl, combine flour, salt and baking powder and mix together. Slowly add the oil and water while mixing with a fork. Continue to mix until dough is smooth, adding small amounts of water and flour if needed.

- When mixture begins to form a ball, set it aside and allow to rest for 15 minutes, covered with a damp towel.

- Transfer the dough from the bowl to a well-floured work surface. Divide it into 20 golf-ball-size amounts, forming each piece into an orb. Flatten to ½-inch thickness. If the dough is sticky, add more flour. When finished, cover flattened balls of dough with a clean kitchen towel and allow to rise for 5 minutes.

- Heat a large pan over medium-high heat. Do not add oil.

- With a rolling pin, roll each dough piece into a rough circle, about 6-7 inches in diameter, keeping your work surface and rolling pin lightly floured. Do not stack uncooked tortillas on top of each other or they will get soggy.

Conclusion

The Never-Ending Story

*N*o truer words have ever been written, as my grain journey is never- ending by design. That is the joy of being a gardener. Hope springs eternal. There will always be another season to look forward to and to learn from. There are will always be new people and conversations that provide valuable insights and inspiration. And a homegrown harvest will always taste better.

As I wrap up this more than two-year process of writing and photographing *Gardening with Grains*, a new season is in front of me. The last of my cool crops are waiting to be harvested and processed while the newly planted warms season grains are just sprouting through the soil. It is bittersweet, to be honest – I am not sure I will ever be ready for this book to be released into the world. I will always want to add new insights and more crops. But, like all things in life, there is a time to finish, and that time is now.

Cultivating grains in my home landscape has changed my life, and I hope they will inspire you in a similar fashion. From that first moment of sowing that gifted bag of wheat seed from my friend Chip, my perspective was broadened. Growing grains has made me a more conscious steward of my little plot of land and of the culinary choices I make every time I eat. They have enhanced my appreciation for farmers, both organic and conventional. Most of all, growing grains has opened my mind to the importance of scientific advancements made by the biotech industry. I no longer see "right or wrong" when discussing food science, but rather focus on practical ways that I can educate others on this convoluted subject.

Every day I wake up excited to share my experiences, in hopes that my successes and failures will help you grow with confidence. I am so grateful to be a horticulturist and home gardener. (I am not even sure I have the capacity to do anything else.) Since my childhood days in 4-H, growing plants has been my passion. I cannot think of another way to spend time that is a greater benefit to the planet. Truly, the act of gardening could save the world!

And that is really the point. Every sunny landscape is an opportunity. With millions of developed acres in North America, it is up to us to see the potential that landscapes offer. Are you satisfied with the status quo? Because, I am not.

I get frustrated when I pass by new construction and see the same landscape mistakes being repeated decade after decade. It saddens me that during my twenty-year career in horticulture the "green layer" is still the last budget consideration. Plants and thoughtful land management can provide essential solutions to the challenges that face our society. From food insecurity to storm water management, plants are the answer!

So much to admire:
a final word in praise of grains

Let me count the ways. As a food crop, cereals are essential to feed the growing human population. In the landscape, they can provide a lot more than just calories. Their roots can reduce erosion and help draw water down into the soil profile. Growing deep into the Earth, they scavenge for nutrients, drawing them back to the surface, providing fertility for the next season. As a natural tiller, grain roots break through hard-packed ground, improving drainage while cleaning storm water runoff. The biomass from grain plants decomposes quickly into organic matter, improving soil quality and increasing microbial activity.

Grains are aesthetically pleasing, with low maintenance needs, no different from the ornamental grasses we all love to grow. But this edible seed can be harvested! Grain seed is inexpensive and abundantly available, making them a practical addition to every landscape, especially new construction, where the ground is in poor condition for planting. When used as a cover crop, grains can heal scarred land and set your future plantings up for long-term success. And of course, the seeds – which can be harvested for your own consumption – will also provide nourishment to local wildlife (think birdseed!).

Inspiring change doesn't happen overnight. This is a grassroots effort to motivate each of you to discover the potential your land offers. I hope you will be motivated to adopt some of the practices described in this book and share your experiences with friends and family. Developing a new garden ethic starts at home, one grain crop at a time. Please encourage your loved ones to get outside and grow something!

Yes, I am the Crazy Grain Lady, and I love gardening with grains. The simplicity of cultivation, the anticipation of harvest, the soil and nutrient benefits, the beauty of the crop: Grains are my muse and have forever changed me as a gardener. Thank you for affording me this opportunity to express my passion. It is a privilege that I cherish every second of the day. I wish you all the best in your own grain journey. ■

Resources

Seed sources I have ordered from over the years:

Baker Creek Heirloom Seed: www.rareseeds.com

Botanical Interests: www.botanicalinterests.com

Grow Organic: www.groworganic.com

Johnny's Seed: www.johnnyseeds.com

Montana Milling: www.montanamilling.com

Park Seed: https://parkseed.com/

Southern Exposure Seed Exchange: www.southernexposure.com

Sustainable Seed Company: https://sustainableseedco.com

Territorial Seeds: www.territorialseed.com

Urban Farmer Seeds: www.ufseeds.com

Victory Seeds: www.victoryseeds.com

Fertilizer I recommend for organic growing:

Espoma Cottonseed Meal: www.espoma.com/product/cottonseed-meal/

Espoma Plant-tone: www.espoma.com/product/plant-tone/

Feather Meal: www.groworganic.com/feather-meal-50-lb.html

Neptune's Harvest Fish Emulsion: www.neptunesharvest.com/

Milling and Processing Equipment:

KitchenAid All Metal Grain Mill: www.kitchenaid.com/countertop-appliances/stand-mixers/attachments/p.all-metal-grain-mill.kgm.html

Wonder Mill: www.thewondermill.com

Manual Grain Grinder: www.walmart.com

Sorghum Press: www.walmart.com

Acknowledgments

There is so much that goes into writing a book, most notably the encouragement given by family, friends, colleagues, mentors and, especially, my kind and patient editor Cathy Dees. Without the support of all the people in my life this book would never have come together. You see, I am a gardener, who happens to write. I will literally find every excuse to not sit in front of a computer, prioritizing ANYTHING that needs to be done outside. And, I am an obsessive photographer, also known as a digital hoarder. If the sun is just right, I will abandon my writing post and get lost looking through the lens for hours at a time.

One of my dearest mentors, Dr. Clifford Parks, used to say, "You are either a gardener or a writer, but very few people are both." That statement rings true for me every day as I struggle to focus on writing but thrive while laboring outside. But, every lesson learned in the garden pushes me to get back on track and share these experiences with others. All in the hopes of rousing your interest and guiding you to success in all that you cultivate.

The impetus for writing this book was born in 2015 thanks to Chip Hope and his generous gift of wheat seed. Inspired by the dynamic grain displays at Chanticleer Garden, it seems I was destined to discover the joys and benefits of grain growing.

Ros Creasy is to be commended for her practical advice on growing that small batch of wheat and ultimately using it to "break bread" with my neighbors so we could all discover the potential that homegrown grains offer. Without her insights and encouragement I may never have eaten that first harvest.

My husband, David Arthur, is really the hero of this story. His unwavering devotion, enthusiastic encouragement, tolerance of my grain obsession and his creative engineering skills have made cultivating and cooking these homegrown grains a reality. Season after season, he never questions my crazy ideas and pushing of limits. From behind the camera to behind the wheelbarrow, David, I am grateful beyond words to be sharing this life with you. Your love and companionship make my life

Rain, shine or hurricane, this crew (Abby, Aidan and David) is dedicated to gardening with grains.

complete, and your creative culinary endeavors nourish my mind, body and spirit.

Gardening is a team effort at my house, along with the best young gardeners anyone could ask for. I am the luckiest person to have the Delgatto family living next door. Aidan and Abby have truly been my right and left hands. In rain, snow, heat and humidity they work tirelessly, helping to cultivate this land. Their observations and genuine interest serve as inspiration for me every day. Thank you for your hard work and devotion.

Professionally, there are so many people who have played a role in making this dream a reality. All of my IPPS mentors, especially Dr. David Creech, Dr. Fred Davies and Dennis Niemeyer, who encourage my passion for plants without fail. Special thanks to North Carolina State University plant breeders Dr. Paul Murphy and Dr. Tom Ranney, whose technical expertise guided me through the confusing and controversial subjects of genetics, modifications and growing ethics. I am especially grateful to all of the event organizers who have welcomed me to their communities with open arms since the debut of *The Foodscape Revolution* in spring of 2017 – and I thank each of you for providing a platform for my career as a garden communicator.

The Gardening with Grains debut

There is one event that stands out – my first presentation of "Gardening with Grains" at the world-class Longwood Gardens in Kennett Square, Pennsylvania. This occasion had been planned for over a year, long before the book was even fully written. If I kept a bucket list, this would have been at the top! It happened to coincide with my 40th birthday, which made it all the more memorable.

Wisely, the program was curated by Matthew Ross, Director of Continuing Education, to include details on designing and growing grains, along with harvesting and processing. A delicious bonus was the live-action five-course tasting menu prepared by Chef Alex Neaton from Longwood's fine dining establishment, 1906. During his cooking demonstration, attendees had the opportunity to sample the vast array of grains they had just learned to grow. With each dish, I watched as everyone discovered the joy of grains. I departed from Longwood that day filled with ambition, dreaming of taking "The Grain Gardener and the Chef" on the road to educate, inspire and whet the appetite of curious people who have probably never grown a cereal crop before.

Admiration and appreciation must be extended to my longtime friend Chef Justin Dillree, who has served as an ingenious culinary force for this book and my go-to pastry chef. Thank you for your friendship, your expertise and for always making the most delicious desserts for all our special occasions. I look forward to what the future holds as we combine our skills and share our passion for grains, both in the garden and in the kitchen.

The beautiful botanical illustrations and landscape drawings are the vision of my gifted friend and landscape architect Preston Montague. Your passion for the natural world and conscientious design skills never cease to amaze me. Thank you for contributing to this effort and for your friendship.

And finally, to the talented team at St. Lynn's Press, for their patience, persistence and professionalism: Paul Kelly, you changed my life when you made me a published author and I will be forever grateful to you. Cathy Dees, your editorial guidance and general wisdom have made me a better person and a much-improved writer. Thank you for believing in me and seeing this through till the end. With thousands of images to choose from, Art Director Holly Rosborough transformed my messy Dropbox files into a tangible, visually inspiring story. Your artistic touches have exceeded my wildest expectations, and I thank you for taking my vision and making it a reality.

Writing a book is a massive feat. Thank you to everyone who provided guidance, motivation, encouragement and consideration. By surrounding myself with intelligent, thoughtful souls, my life is extraordinary and I am grateful, always. ∎

About the Author

Brie Arthur is widely recognized as one of the charismatic young leaders who are helping to determine the future of the horticulture industry and the way we think about gardens and gardening. Her bestselling first book, *The Foodscape Revolution* (2017, St. Lynn's Press), showed us how to take ornamental gardening up a notch: growing fruits and veggies alongside traditional plantings and doing it with pizzazz and purpose.

Gardening with Grains is her latest passion project, born from an aha realization that we've been missing a dynamic piece of the burgeoning foodscape movement: grains – those ancient and beautiful grasses that practically *gave* us civilization. Brie's core belief is that all things horticultural are the way to create a healthier future for the world.

Brie studied Landscape Design and Horticulture at Purdue University and has worked as a propagator and grower at leading nurseries. In 2017, she was awarded the first "Emerging Professional" distinction by the American Horticultural Society for her efforts in connecting a new generation to the art of growing. Brie is president of the International Plant Propagators Society, Southern Region.

She appears as a correspondent on the PBS television show "Growing a Greener World" and shares real-life gardening advice through her YouTube channel, Brie Grows.

Along with her husband, David, and kitties Acer, Kubby and Sophia, Brie gardens on the "sandy side" of Wake County, North Carolina. Within the boundaries of their one-acre suburban lot, she tends a diverse collection of trees, shrubs, perennials and seasonal annuals – both for beauty and bounty. Combined with David's cooking skills, they enjoy a homegrown gardener-and-chef lifestyle and hope to develop a garden retreat center in the future so they can both share their skills and love for everything that plants offer! ■

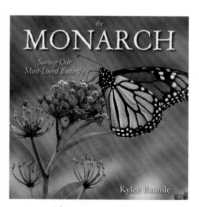